FOREWORD BY RAY

the
MIRACLE MORNING
FOR NETWORK MARKETERS

GROW YOURSELF **FIRST** TO
GROW YOUR BUSINESS **FAST**

HAL ELROD | PAT PETRINI
WITH HONORÉE CORDER

THE MIRACLE MORNING FOR NETWORK MARKETERS
Hal Elrod

Interior Design: 3CsBooks.com

WHAT OTHER NETWORK MAREKTING EXPERTS ARE SAYING...

"After meeting hundreds of successful network marketing professionals from all over the world, we have noticed one common trait and is this: they all have an ongoing and consistent focus on their personal development. They never stop learning or growing. In most professions, you get up and go to work. In network marketing, you get up and you go to work on yourself. This book is a fantastic tool to teach you how to become someone who doesn't wish or hope to be that person. It will teach you how to do it. Cannot recommend it enough"

—Richard Fenton and Andrea Waltz, Authors, *Go for No!*

"I first shared the stage with Pat Petrini when he was an up-and-coming networking professional. He has become one of the true professionals in our industry and he has a unique ability to make complicated concepts immediately understandable and applicable. With *The Miracle Morning for Network Marketers*, he has knocked it out of the park. It marries the incredibly powerful concept of the Miracle Morning with the teaching of the fundamental skills that every networker needs to master in order to really make it in our profession. Put this on your 'must read' list!"

—Doug Wead, Professional Network Marketer, New York Times Best-Selling Author & Former White House Advisor

"I can't recommend this book highly enough. If every network marketer actually applied the lessons taught in this book, the benefit to the network marketing world would be immeasurable. Game-changer!"

—Ted Nuyten, CEO of BusinessForHome.org

"The Miracle Morning for Network Marketers is, hands down, the best book that I have ever read. Period."

—Pat Petrini's mom, Colleen Petrini

A Special Invitation from Hal

Readers and practitioners of *The Miracle Morning* have co-created an extraordinary community consisting of over 200,000 like-minded individuals from around the world who wake up each day with purpose and dedicate time to fulfilling the unlimited potential that is within all of us, while helping others to do the same.

As author of *The Miracle Morning*, I felt I had a responsibility to create an online community where readers could come together to connect, get encouragement, share best practices, support one another, discuss the book, post videos, find accountability partners, and even swap smoothie recipes and exercise routines.

However, I honestly had no idea that The Miracle Morning Community would become one of the most positive, engaged, and supportive online communities in the world—but it has. I'm constantly astounded by the caliber and character of our membership, which presently includes people from over 70 countries and is growing daily.

Just go to **www.MyTMMCommunity.com** and request to join The Miracle Morning Community on Facebook®. You'll immediately be able to connect with 80,000+ people who are already practicing TMM. While you'll find many who are just beginning their Miracle Morning journey, you'll discover even more who have been at it for years and who will happily share advice and guidance to accelerate your success.

I'll be moderating the Community and checking in regularly, so I look forward to seeing you there! If you'd like to reach out to me personally on social media, follow **@HalElrod** on Twitter and **Facebook.com/YoPalHal** on Facebook. Let's connect soon!

Bulk Discount Program

When writing this book, I asked myself "what information do I want in the hands of every new marketer that joins my team?" The chapters you see before you are the result.

With that in mind, I wanted to make it easy (and cheaper) for you to supply your team members with a copy of this book, should you feel it would add value to them.

If you would like to make copies available for purchase at your events or to your team members, you can contact us directly and we will work with you on pricing depending on the quantity that you wish to purchase.

Contact us at
support@TMMforNetworkMarketers.com

DEDICATION

HAL

This book is dedicated to the most important people in my life—my family. To my loving and supportive wife-for-life, Ursula, and our two children, Sophie and Halsten. I love you all more than I can put into words.

PAT

I would like to thank Vector Marketing and Cutco Cutlery. My sales training there started me down the paths of entrepreneurship and personal development that have led directly to the opportunities that I have today.

I'd also like to thank Bob Schmidt, who taught a 22-year-old kid how to grow a team and live the life of his dreams through network marketing.

Most importantly, my parents and my wife, Emily, who is both the hottest and the coolest chick on the planet! She's my perfect partner and always supports me in all the crazy projects I take on. I love you!

CONTENTS

FOREWORD
BY RAY HIGDON

Dear Reader,

My morning routine is sacred (just ask my wife)! I don't start any day without doing a few key practices that set the tone for my day, and therefore, my life.

In fact, I fully attribute my morning routine as the BIGGEST key to the millions that I have made as a Network Marketer over the last few years. What you hold in your hands right now has the power to change your life, and business, for the better, forever… if you allow it.

Why is a morning routine so important? Why not a night routine? Why not a mid-afternoon routine? Quite simply, because you can control your day by taking control of your morning. By the time night rolls around, your attitude and energy will have been affected by the day's events. By taking control of your day, first thing in the morning, you take control of your energy and attitude, and therefore your results.

By 8:30 a.m., I have typically already accomplished the following:

- Exercised
- Meditated
- Completed my gratitude practice

- Written a blog post
- Recorded a podcast
- Responded to all emails and social media interactions.

Then I have the rest of my day to work on my big goals and dreams! I'm in a positive frame of mind, I've accomplished tasks that move the needle in my mind and in my business -- I'm off to a terrific start to my day, every single day.

What if YOU became that productive? Well, you can, and Hal Elrod and Pat Petrini are just the guys to get you where you want to go. The Miracle Morning for Network Marketers is your roadmap to success!

I encourage you to truly immerse yourself in this book. Read it, but also seek to adhere to its principles.

Here's to you creating the life of your dreams by simply taking control of how you start each day from this day forward.

Ray Higdon, Network Marketing Trainer, Speaker and Coach

www.RayHigdon.com

INTRODUCTION
MY MIRACLE MORNING

"What greater wealth is there than to own your life and to spend it on growing? Every living thing must grow. It can't stand still. It must grow or perish."
—AYN RAND, Atlas Shrugged

I've been getting high a LOT lately ...

Seriously, on a daily basis, I am intentionally flooding my brain with dopamine, serotonin, and other neurotransmitters that make me feel amazing, help me focus, and juice up my creativity and productivity. What is my stimulant of choice? It's my Miracle Morning.

It's hard to describe. I've always been a pretty positive person. I've always been a hard worker. I've even managed to put a few business successes under my belt. However, since I began implementing The Miracle Morning, my life has been elevated to a whole new level.

In *The 7 Habits of Highly Effective People*, Stephen Covey talks about the importance of prioritizing the activities that are important but not urgent. He defines important activities as the things that are critical to accomplishing your long-term goals, but have no inherent deadline; they are easy to put off in lieu of more urgent (and less important) tasks.

The usual suspects are working out, reading, prospecting, following up, etc. The activities that, if done every day, will absolutely have the greatest impact on your life, but that are easy to reschedule because the car broke down.

Now, every day when my Miracle Morning is complete, I've already checked a lot of those items off of my list, my brain is surging with happy chemicals, I feel amazing, and I'm energized to attack my to-do list for the day. It's the same feeling I often get after a rousing motivational talk, or after watching *Braveheart*. It used to be a feeling that popped up unannounced for me, seemingly at random. But now, I intentionally manufacture that feeling at will, and I do it every day with my Miracle Morning.

I'm hooked. Like a drug addict whose life is spiraling upward instead of downward. And, my singular goal in co-authoring this book is to get you hooked as well.

Just try it. All the cool kids are doing it!

By the way, if you would like to see my current Miracle Morning routine, go to www.PatPetrini.com/MiracleMorning.

How We Got Here

Hal and I first met when we were teenagers working as sales reps for the same company. I had broken a few sales records and was the #1 sales rep in the company at one point while Hal had broken a *lot* of records and went on to become a Hall of Fame Sales Representative and one of the most sought-after trainers in the company.

In 2004, at the age of 22, I was introduced to the concept of network marketing. The lure of residual income was too much for me to resist. I left my sales position to focus on network marketing. Hal eventually started down his path of becoming a top business coach, keynote speaker, and bestselling author.

I had dreams of building a massive organization and traveling the world while the checks just rolled in. And, they came true ... eventually.

My first experience with network marketing was the same story that you often hear. I spent a ton of money ordering a ton of product, I worked my butt off, and I netted a grand total of $60 in commissions over the course of six months. Needless to say, the difference between what I had earned and what I believed I was capable of earning was significant.

Everything changed when I met a man named Bob Schmidt. Bob had been a professional network marketer for decades by the time we were introduced. He had been with four companies in his career and had earned his way to being one of the top three earners in each of those companies. He'd made tens of millions of dollars in his career, was responsible for over $1 billion in product sales, and had zero patience for anybody that came off as a whiner, complainer, or excuse-maker.

I joined Bob in the fourth and final company he built before he passed a few years later. I studied his presentations. I listened in on his three-way phone calls. In the car between appointments, I listened to his trainings and the books he recommended. I did my best to implement and take action on everything that I was learning from him, *and it worked!*

Within one year, my residual income was enough for me to live on comfortably (that doesn't take a lot when you are 23 years old!). Within two years, I had a nice six-figure income, was traveling the world, and living very comfortably on half of my income while saving and investing the rest. For me, the dream had become a reality.

So what changed? Two things:

1. Somebody who knew what they were doing (Bob) told me what to do.

2. I did what they told me to do.

That's it. That's the formula. It is my hope that this book can help you with #1. It's up to you to do #2.

Fast forward a few years, and I have had the great fortune of becoming a million-dollar earner in network marketing, a consultant to network marketing companies, and (fun fact) the creator of the most viral video in all of network marketing (check it out at www. MLMcartoon.com).

I'll admit I had heard about *The Miracle Morning* years ago when Hal first wrote the book, but I said "Nope! I'm definitely not a morning person," and continued my normal routine while watching Hal build *The Miracle Morning* brand from a distance.

Eventually, The Miracle Morning started going viral. I saw people I know post about and how it had changed their lives. Hal was starting to show up as a guest speaker on some of the podcasts I listened to. I thought *this Miracle Morning thing seems to really be catching on ... good for Hal!*

Then, Hal reached out to me and asked if I would be interested in co-authoring this book, *The Miracle Morning for Network Marketers,* and I thought, *well, I guess I better read it!*

Needless to say, I read it. I loved it. I implemented it. And that is how I became the addict that I am today!

The Miracle Morning for Network Marketers

In writing this book, I interviewed dozens of top network marketers, all of whom are in the top 1 percent of their respective companies. I wanted to uncover what they did differently than— and with the same amount of time as—the other 99 percent, and those distinctions are covered in the chapters to come. The average income of these individuals ranges from $250,000 to millions of dollars annually.

The more I studied the world's top network marketers, the more I came to realize that the majority of their success in business is a result of *who they are*, not just what they do. I've written this book because I want you to have both—to simultaneously master every aspect of successful selling while you master every facet of *yourself.*

And therein lies the premise, and promise, of this book: If you want to take your *network marketing business* to the next level, you must first figure out how to take *yourself* to the next level.

If you want to attract, create, and sustain extraordinary levels of success and income, you must first figure out how to become the person that is capable of easily and consistently attracting, creating, and sustaining the extraordinary levels of success and income that you desire.

Then, you must master what the top network marketers know about building a business that provides the freedom and income only the top 1 percent enjoy. You need to learn the intricacies and nuances of the business—things like prospecting, presenting opportunity and products, following up, and finally, getting new marketers started in your organization.

The Miracle Morning for Network Marketers is not like any other book on network marketing. It's *the* reference book that reveals how to succeed in *every* area of your life, simultaneously; how to be a top network marketer *and* experience a life of health, balance, and fulfillment. This is a book that tells you what the top network marketers do, and it gives you an edge, right from the start, by helping you to become one of them—mentally, emotionally, spiritually, skillfully, *and* strategically.

It's Your Turn

What if you could wake up tomorrow morning with absolute faith that the day was going to be awesome? What if waking up early was a habit you absolutely loved? What if every morning could be like Christmas morning—you know, the really awesome Christmas mornings of your childhood? When you went to bed full of anticipation of what was going to happen the next day, and woke up so excited you woke your parents up at 4 a.m. to get on with the business of ripping open all of your gifts. (Or was that just me?) Any interest?

I can assure you that's exactly how I feel each and every day. I go to bed looking forward to the next day and wake up each morning anticipating what the day has in store for me. I'm utterly grateful my life has transformed into something so amazing.

I know. You might be thinking, *I've tried and failed. I've tried to get up earlier. I've tried to master my life and my professional growth.*

I have failed more times than I care to admit, and I'm nervous about trying something new. Can this really help me?

Yes! Yes! *Yes!*

I've experienced both sides of the coin. I know what it's like to struggle to meet my goals, and I know what it's like to succeed beyond my wildest dreams. Even writing this book wouldn't have crossed my mind a few short years ago.

I know what it's like to search for greener grass, and I know what it's like to have the lawn that my colleagues and competitors envy and causes them to ask me for my secret sauce. This book *is* my secret sauce. I've included every single distinction, action, and hack I use to stay at the top of my network marketing game, and my life.

More importantly, I believe you're ready. Ready to take yourself, your network marketing business, and your life to levels that, deep down, you know you're capable of, *or you wouldn't be reading this book.* The principles within this book can be the means to realize your dreams, and to start building the business and earning the money you've only dreamed about. The kind of money that will allow you to move beyond the stress that small and inconsistent bonus checks cause and into a life and business that enables you to live the life of your dreams.

I believe that to be truly successful, in whatever way you measure success, you must master both your inner and outer game. It all starts with the morning. When you own the morning, you own the day. And when you own the day, you can own your network marketing business. When that happens, *you own your life.* I know if it was and is possible for me to do it, it is possible *for you to do it, too.*

If you let it, *The Miracle Morning for Network Marketers* can be your coach, accountability partner, and mastermind team all rolled into one. I want it to be your constant companion until your network marketing career has been so completely transformed that you almost can't remember what it was like when you started. Keep this book and your journal close at hand so you can refer to it, make notes, jot down the distinctions you make, and track your progress.

You can be just as successful, if not more so, than I have been. You can take the success I've enjoyed and multiply it for yourself.

All you have to do to start is take control of your morning.

Are you ready?

— 1 —
WHY MORNINGS MATTER
(MORE THAN YOU THINK)

"Instead of wondering when your next vacation is, maybe you should set up a life you don't need to escape from."

–SETH GODIN, New York Times
Best-Selling Author

How you start each morning sets your mindset, and the context, for the rest of your day. Start every day with a purposeful, disciplined, growth-infused, and goal-oriented morning, and you're virtually guaranteed to crush your day.

Yet most network marketers start their days with procrastination, hitting the snooze button, and sending a message to their subconscious that says they don't have enough self-discipline to get out of bed in the morning, let alone do what's necessary to reach their business growth goals.

When the alarm clock starts beeping in the morning, consider it to be akin to life's first gift to us. It's the gift of time to dedicate to becoming the person you need to be to achieve all of your goals and dreams while the rest of the world is still asleep.

You might be thinking, *All of this sounds great, Pat. But. I. Am. Not. A. Morning. Person.*

I understand. I really do! You're not saying anything I haven't told myself a thousand times before. And believe me, I tried—and failed—many times to take control of my mornings. But that was before I discovered *The Miracle Morning.*

Stay with me for a minute. In addition to wanting to have one of the biggest organizations in your company, I bet you also want to stop struggling and worrying about having more month than money, quit missing your goals, and release all of the intense and not-so-great emotions that go along with those challenges. Right?

Then know this:

Mornings are the key to all of it.

More important than even the *time* that you start your day is the *mindset* with which you start your day.

Maybe your dream is to build passive income with network marketing so that you can inspect your alarm clock's insides with a baseball bat and see what it's like to start your day on *your* time for a while.

Trust me, I get it, and I often decide to start my day whenever I wake up naturally. However, even when I do that, my Miracle Morning is the first part of my day and gets me in the right mindset to make the most of the rest of my day.

Plus, there is a good chance that you might be reading this book in the early stages of your network marketing business, which means that you are probably paying your bills with your day job and building your network marketing business on the side. If that's the case, then learning to implement your Miracle Morning with your day job is going to be critical to really exploding your network marketing business so that you can finally ditch that alarm clock for a few weekdays (or forever) and see how it feels. Here's the good news ... It's worth it, and it is far more fun and rewarding than you might expect.

But, before we get into exactly *how* you can master your mornings, let me make the case for *why*. Because believe me, once you know the truth about mornings, you'll never want to miss one again.

Why Mornings Matter So Much

The more you dig into mornings, the more the proof mounts that the early bird gets a *lot* more than the worm. Here are just a few of the key advantages to laying off the snooze button.

You'll be more proactive. Christoph Randler is a professor of biology at the University of Education in Heidelberg, Germany. In the July 2010 issue of *Harvard Business Review*, Randler found that "People whose performance peaks in the morning are better positioned for career success, because they're more proactive than people who are at their best in the evening."

You'll anticipate problems and head them off at the pass. Randler went on to surmise that morning people hold all of the important cards. They are "better able to anticipate and minimize problems, are proactive, have greater professional success and ultimately make higher wages." He noted that morning people are able to anticipate problems and handle them with grace and ease, which makes them better in business.

You'll plan like a pro. Morning folks have the time to organize, anticipate, and plan for their day. Our sleepy counterparts are reactive rather than proactive, leaving a lot to chance. Aren't you more stressed when you sleep through your alarm or when you wake up late? Getting up with the sun (or before) lets you get a jump start on the day. While everyone else is running around trying (and failing) to get their day under control, you'll be calm, cool, and collected.

You'll have more energy. One of the components of your new *Miracle Mornings* will be morning exercise, which—in as little as just a few minutes a day—sets a positive tone for the day. Increased blood to the brain will help you think more clearly and focus on what's most important. Fresh oxygen will permeate every cell in your body and increase your energy all day, which is why top network marketers who exercise report being in a better mood and in better shape, getting better sleep, and being more productive.

This, of course, will result in your producing significant increases in your numbers. You'll acquire more customers, enroll more business builders, and earn bigger bonus checks!

You'll gain early bird attitude advantages ... Recently, researchers at the University of Barcelona in Spain, compared morning people, those early birds who like to get up at dawn, with evening people, night owls who prefer to stay up late and sleep in. Among the differences, they found that morning people tend to be more persistent and resistant to fatigue, frustration, and difficulties. That translates into lower levels of anxiety and lower rates of depression, higher life satisfaction, and less likelihood of substance abuse. Sounds good to me.

... and you'll avoid night owl disadvantages. On the other hand, evening people tend to be more extravagant, temperamental, impulsive, and novelty-seeking, "with a higher tendency to explore the unknown." They are more likely to suffer from insomnia and ADHD. They also appear to be more likely to develop addictive behaviors, mental disorders, and antisocial tendencies—and even to attempt suicide. Not a pretty picture.

The evidence is in, and the experts have had their say. *Mornings contain the secret to an extraordinarily successful future in network marketing.*

Mornings? Really?

I'll admit it. To go from *I'm not a morning person* to *I really want to become a morning person* to *I'm up early every morning, and it's pretty flippin' amazing!* is a process. But after some trial and error, you will discover how to out-fox, pre-empt, and foil your inner late sleeper so you can make early rising a habit. Okay, sounds great in theory, but you might be shaking your head and telling yourself, *There's no way. I'm already cramming twenty-seven hours of stuff into twenty-four hours. How on earth could I get up an hour earlier than I already do?* I ask the question, "How can you not?"

The key thing to understand is that *The Miracle Morning* isn't about trying to deny yourself another hour of sleep so you can have an even longer, harder day. It's not even about waking up earlier. It's about waking up *better*.

Thousands of people around the planet are already living their own Miracle Mornings. Many of them were night owls. But they're making it work. In fact, they're *thriving*. And it's not because they simply added an hour to their day. It's because they added *the right* hour. And so can you.

Still skeptical? Then believe this: **The hardest part about getting up an hour earlier is the first five minutes.** That's the crucial time when—tucked into your warm bed—you make the decision to start your day or hit the snooze button *just one more time*. It's the moment of truth, and the decision you make right then will change your day, your success, and your life.

And that's why that first five minutes is the starting point for *The Miracle Morning for Network Marketers*. It's time for you to win every morning!

In the next two chapters, I'll make waking up early easier and more exciting than it's ever been in your life (even if you've *never* considered yourself to be a morning person), and I'll show you how to maximize those newfound morning minutes.

Chapters 4, 5, and 6 will reveal not-so-obvious network marketing principles related to accelerating your personal growth, why you need to strategically engineer your life for endless amounts of energy, and how to optimize your ability to stay focused on your goals and what matters most.

Finally, chapters 7, 8, 9, and 10 cover the critical skills you must master to become a successful network marketer, elevate your business, and increase your income as fast as humanly possible. There's even a final bonus chapter from Hal that I think you are really going to love!

We have a lot of ground to cover in this book, so let's jump right in.

TOP ONE PERCENT NETWORKER INTERVIEW

Ray Higdon

www.RayHigdon.com

Facebook.com/rayhigdonpage

Periscope: @RayHigdon

YouTube.com/user/rayhigdon1

A few of Ray's accomplishments:

- Two time best-selling author.

- #1 income earner in previous network marketing company.

- Podcast has over 1.5 million downloads.

- His blog gets 100,000 unique visitors per month.

- Went from Foreclosure to millionaire in 4 years.

Ray's Miracle Morning & Daily Rituals:

• Before I go to bed I set my phone on airplane mode, they say it's a good health practice and I read my daily affirmations that are located on my phone. To do this I just wrote them down on flashcards and I took pictures of them and stored them in an album. I start my day by reading these on my phone.

• I weigh myself. It's good to weigh yourself as what is tracked can get improved AND if you are going to weigh yourself you should do it at the same time each day and wearing the same thing.

• Rinse my Mouth and Brush my Teeth (ok, maybe I could have skipped telling you this step but just being thorough!) My dentist told me Sonicare was the best so that is what I use.

• I drink water, lots of it. Sometimes I will squirt some lemon in there, sometimes not. I drink at least two of these right away, they are 26oz. This is a BPA free plastic cup. Before I am done with breakfast I will have drank four of these (over 100 oz's of water))

- I head to my gym and do 30 minutes on the Exercise bike. It is at THIS point that I "un-airplane" mode my phone and I check my social media accounts and my email while doing the exercise bike. I LOVE doing more than one thing at a time, NO ONE should check their phone in the morning while not on a treadmill, walking or on an exercise bike.

- I make a green drink for me and my wife. My wife is NEVER up yet but I make it for her and she mixes it up when she does wake up. The ingredients are cabbage, kale, spinach, lemon, celery and cucumber. It doesn't taste fantastic to me but it isn't bad. I use THE best blender on the planet, the Vitamix.

- I eat two eggs with high mineral sea salt.

- I enter my "gratitude grotto" (hot tub) and spend 10-15 minutes just being grateful for everything in my life and for an amazing day about to happen.

- THEN I get to work. Usually it is getting a blog post done, sometimes it is shooting a video for the blog or clients and look over what my schedule is like that day and what needs to happen on our different projects. We use basecamp to manage all our projects and I make sure no one is waiting for me on anything and every single day, all of the above and my blog post is done by 8:30am

BONUS INTERVIEW FOR *MIRACLE MORNING FOR NETWORK MARKETING* READERS

Each of the Top One Percent Networkers that are featured in this book were interviewed by Pat Petrini about not only their morning routines, but their tips, techniques and strategies that have been critical in helping them become the best of the best in network marketing.

For your free and exclusive interview with Ray, go to
www.TMMforNetworkMarketers.com/Ray

TOP ONE PERCENT NETWORKER INTERVIEW

Maria Williams

Facebook.com/NrF2Activator

Maria began as a poor Brazilian immigrant with BIG dreams. She was the first in her family to graduate college with a BA from The University of Massachusetts.

She worked for 20 years successfully in human resources and then, in 2008, the economy forced her family to make a move to Arizona and she was in search of more flexible work options. That is how she found network marketing.

In just 5 short years, her organization has generated over $9 million in product sales with 36,000 people on her team and growing every day.

Maria's Miracle Morning & Daily Rituals:

- Before opening my eyes, I say my prayers, thank God for another amazing day, thank Him for blessing me and my family and ask God to guide me through the day and help my team.
- I make breakfast and get my family on their merry way.
- Glance at texts, email and schedule so I don't miss anything.
- Workout for 45 min to 1 hr - run with dogs or gym with personal trainer.
- Double check the day's appointments - I live by my calendar. I schedule everything so I can attain a sane balance in life. It's been hard to say 'no' to people but if it is not scheduled, it is not happening.
- Listen to at least 20 minutes of self improvement audio sessions.

- Read at least 30 minutes to feed my brain and heart daily with positive motivational stuff.
- Do a good deed for somebody - Pay it forward.

BONUS INTERVIEW FOR *MIRACLE MORNING FOR NETWORK MARKETING* READERS

Each of the Top One Percent Networkers that are featured in this book were interviewed by Pat Petrini about not only their morning routines, but their tips, techniques and strategies that have been critical in helping them become the best of the best in network marketing.

For your free and exclusive interview with Maria, go to www.TMMforNetworkMarketers.com/Maria

— 2 —
IT ONLY TAKES FIVE MINUTES TO BECOME A MORNING PERSON

If you really think about it, hitting the snooze button in the morning doesn't even make sense. It's like saying, "I hate getting up in the morning, so I do it over, and over, and over again."
—DEMETRI MARTIN, Stand-up Comedian

It is possible to love waking up—even if you've *never* been a morning person.

I know you might not believe it. Right now you might think, *that might be true for early birds, but trust me, I've tried. I'm just not a morning person.*

But it's true. I know because I've been there. I was a bleary-eyed, snooze-button pusher. A "snooze-aholic" as Hal calls it. I was a morning dreader. I hated waking up.

And now I love it.

How did I do it? When people ask me how I transformed myself into a morning person—and transformed my life in the process—I tell them I did it in five simple steps, one at a time. I know it may seem downright impossible. But take it from a former snooze-aholic: you can do this. And you can do it the same way that I did.

That's the critical message about waking up—it's possible to change. Morning people aren't born—they're self-made. You can become a morning person, and you can do it in simple steps that don't require the willpower of an Olympic marathoner. I contend that when early rising becomes not something you do but *who you are* you will truly love mornings. Waking up will become for you like it is for me, effortless.

Not convinced? Suspend your disbelief just a little and let me introduce you to the five-step process that changed my life. Five simple, snooze-proof keys that made waking up in the morning— even early in the morning—easier than ever before. Without this strategy, I would still be sleeping (or snoozing) through my alarm(s) each morning. Worse, I would still be clinging to the limiting belief that I was not a morning person.

And I would have missed a whole world of opportunity.

The Challenge with Waking Up

Waking up earlier is a bit like trying a new diet: It's easy to get pumped up about all the great results you're going to get, starting tomorrow.

But when tomorrow comes? And you're hungry? And your favorite food is staring up at you from the fridge or the café menu?

Well, we all know what happens then. Good intentions fly out the window. Motivation goes into hibernation. And the next thing you know, you're curled up with a tub of ice cream.

Mornings are not so different. Right now, I bet you're plenty motivated. But what happens tomorrow morning when that alarm goes off? How motivated will you be when you're yanked out of a deep sleep in a warm bed by a screaming alarm clock in a cold house?

I think we both know where motivation will be right then. It will have gone off-shift and been replaced by rationalization. And rationalization is a crafty master—in just seconds we can convince ourselves that we need just a few extra minutes …

… and the next thing we know we're scrambling around the house late for work. Again.

It's a tricky problem. Just when we need our motivation the most—those first few moments of the day—is precisely when we seem to have the least of it.

The solution, then, is to boost that morning motivation, to mount a surprise attack on rationalization. That's what the five steps that follow do. Each step in the process is designed to do one thing: increase what I call your Wake-Up Motivation Level (WUML).

First thing in the morning, you might have a low WUML, meaning you want nothing more than to go back to sleep when your alarm goes off. That's normal. But by using this process, you can reach a high WUML, where you're ready to jump up and embrace the day.

The Five-Minute Snooze-Proof Wake-Up Strategy

Minute One: Set Your Intentions Before Bed

The first key to waking up is to remember this: Your first thought in the morning is usually the last thought you had before you went to bed. I bet, for example, that you've had nights where you could hardly fall asleep because you were so excited about waking up the next morning. Whether it was Christmas morning or the start of a big vacation, as soon as the alarm clock sounded you opened your eyes ready to jump out of bed and embrace the day. Why? It's because the last thought you had about the coming morning before you went to bed was positive.

On the other hand, if your last thought before bed was something like, *Oh man, I can't believe I have to get up in six hours—I'm going to be exhausted in the morning!* then your first thought when the alarm clock goes off is likely to be something like, *Oh my gosh, it's already been six hours? Nooo! I just want to keep sleeping!*

The first step, then, is to consciously decide every night to actively and mindfully create a positive expectation for the next morning.

For help on this and to get the precise words to say before bed to create your powerful intentions, download *The Miracle Morning Bedtime Affirmations* free at www.TMMBook.com.

Minute Two: Walk *Across The Room* To Turn Off The Alarm

If you haven't already, move your alarm clock across the room. This forces you to get out of bed and engage your body in movement. Motion creates energy—getting all the way up and out of bed naturally helps you wake up.

If you keep your alarm clock next to your bed, you're still in a partial sleep state when the alarm goes off, and it makes it much more difficult to wake yourself up. In fact, you may have turned off the alarm without even realizing it! On more than a few occasions, you might have even convinced yourself that your alarm clock was merely part of the dream you were having. (You're not alone on that one; trust me.)

Simply forcing yourself to get out of bed to turn off the alarm clock will instantly increase your WUML. However, you'll likely still be feeling more sleepy than not. So to raise that WUML just a little further, try …

Minute Three: Brush Your Teeth

As soon as you've gotten out of bed and turned off your alarm clock, go directly to the bathroom sink to brush your teeth. While you're at it, splash some water on your face. This simple activity will increase your WUML even further.

Now that your mouth is fresh, it's time to …

Minute Four: Drink a Full Glass of Water

It's crucial that you hydrate yourself first thing every morning. After six to eight hours without water, you'll be mildly dehydrated, which causes fatigue. Often when people feel tired—at any time of the day—what they really need is more water, not more sleep.

Start by getting a glass or bottle of water (or you can do what I do, and fill it up the night before so it's already there for you in the morning), and drink it as fast as is comfortable for you. The objective is to replace the water you were deprived of during the hours you slept. (And hey, the side benefits of morning hydration are better, younger-looking skin and even maintaining a healthy weight. Not bad for a few ounces of water!)

That glass of water should raise your WUML another notch, which will get you to …

Minute Five: Get Dressed or Jump in the Shower

The fifth step has two options. Option one is to get dressed in your exercise clothes, so you're ready to leave your bedroom and immediately engage in your *Miracle Morning*. You can either lay out your clothes before you go to bed or even sleep in your work-out clothes. (Yes, really.)

Option two is to jump in the shower. I usually change into exercise clothes, since I'll need a shower after working out, but a lot of people prefer the morning shower because it helps them wake up and gives them a fresh start to the day. The choice is yours.

Regardless of which option you choose, by the time you've executed these five simple steps, your WUML should be high enough that it requires very little discipline to stay awake for your *Miracle Morning*.

If you were to try and make that commitment at the moment your alarm clock first went off—while you were at a WUML of nearly zero—it would be a much more difficult decision to make. The five steps let you build momentum so that within just a few minutes you're ready to go instead of feeling groggy.

Miracle Morning Bonus Wake-Up Tips

Although this strategy has worked for thousands of people, these five steps are not the only way to make waking up in the morning easier. Here are a few other tips I've heard from fellow Miracle Morning practitioners:

- *The Miracle Morning* "Bedtime Affirmations": If you haven't done this yet, be sure to take a moment now to go to www. TMMbook.com and download the re-energizing, intention-setting "Bedtime Affirmations," for free. There is nothing more effective for ensuring you will wake up before your alarm than programming your mind to achieve exactly what you want.

- Set a timer for your bedroom lights: One of The Miracle Morning Community members sets his bedroom lights on a timer (you can buy an appliance timer online or at your local hardware store). As his alarm goes off, the lights come on in the room. What a great idea! It's a lot easier to fall back asleep when it's dark—having the lights on tells your mind and body that it's time to wake up. (Regardless of whether you use a timer, be sure to turn your light on first thing when your alarm goes off.)

- Set a timer for your bedroom heater: Another fan of *The Miracle Morning* says that in the winter, she keeps a bedroom heater on an appliance timer set to go off fifteen minutes before she wakes up. She keeps it cold at night, but warm for waking up so that she won't be tempted to crawl back under her covers.

Feel free to add to or customize the Five-Minute Snooze-Proof Wake-Up Strategy, and if you have any tips you're open to sharing, we'd love to hear them. Please share them in The Miracle Morning Community at www.MyTMMCommunity.com.

Waking up consistently and easily is all about having an effective, pre-determined, step-by-step strategy to increase your WUML in the morning. Don't wait to try this! Start tonight by reading *The Miracle Morning* "Bedtime Affirmations," moving your alarm clock across the room, setting a glass of water on your nightstand, and committing to the other two steps for the morning.

How to Go From Unbearable to Unstoppable (In 30 Days)

Incorporating any new habit requires an adjustment period—don't expect this to be effortless from day one. But do make a commitment to yourself to stick with it. The seemingly unbearable first few days are only temporary. While there's a lot of debate around how long it takes to create a new habit, 30 days is definitely enough to test-drive your new morning routine.

Here's what you might expect as you build your new routine.

Phase One: Unbearable (Days 1–10)

Phase One is when any new activity requires tremendous effort, and getting up early is no different. You're fighting existing habits, the very habits that have often been entrenched in *who you are* for years.

In this phase, it's mind over matter—and if you don't mind, it'll definitely matter! The habits of hitting snooze and not making the most of your day are the same habits that are holding you back from becoming the superstar network marketer you have always known you can be, so dig in and hold strong.

In Phase One, while you battle existing patterns and limiting beliefs, you'll find out what you're made of and what you're capable of. You need to keep pushing, stay committed to your vision, and hang in there. Trust me when I say you can do this!

I know it can be daunting on day five to realize you still have twenty-five days to go before your transformation is complete and you've become a bona fide morning person. Keep in mind that on day five, you're actually more than halfway through the first phase and well on your way. Remember: your initial feelings are not going to last forever. In fact, you owe it to yourself to persevere because in no time at all, you'll be getting the exact results you want as you become the person you've always wanted to be!

Phase Two: Uncomfortable (Days 11–20)

In Phase Two, your body and mind begin to acclimate to waking up earlier. You'll notice that getting up earlier starts to get a tiny bit easier, but it's not yet a habit—it's not quite who you are and likely won't feel natural yet.

The biggest temptation at this level is to reward yourself by taking a break, especially on the weekends. A question posted quite often in The Miracle Morning Community is, "How many days a week do you get up early for your Miracle Morning?" My answer— and the one that's most common from long-time Miracle Morning practitioners is *every single day*.

Once you've made it through Phase One, you've made it through the hardest period. So keep going! Why on earth would you want to go through that first phase again by taking one or two days off? Trust me, you wouldn't, so don't!

Phase Three: Unstoppable (Days 21–30)

Early rising is now not only a habit, it has literally become part of *who you are*, part of your identity. Your body and mind will have become accustomed to your new way of being. These next ten days are important for cementing the habit in yourself and your life.

As you engage in *The Miracle Morning* practice, you will also develop an appreciation for the three distinct phases of habit change. A side benefit is you will realize you can identify, develop, and adopt any habit that serves you—up to and including the habits of the top performers I have included in this book.

What Do I DO With My Morning?

Thirty days, you might be thinking, *I can get up earlier for thirty days … But what do I DO with that time?*

This is where the magic begins. I'm going to introduce you to the routines at the heart of *The Miracle Morning*. They're called the Life S.A.V.E.R.S., and they're the habits that are going to transform your mornings, your career, and your life!

Taking Immediate Action:

There's no need to wait to get started with creating your new, amazing future. As Anthony Robbins has said, "When is NOW a good time for you to do that?" Now, indeed, would be perfect! In fact, the sooner you start, the sooner you'll begin to see results, including increased energy, a better attitude, and, of course, more success with your network marketing business.

Step One: Set your alarm for one hour earlier than you usually wake up, and schedule that hour in your calendar to do your first *Miracle Morning* ... tomorrow morning.

From this day forward, starting with the next 30 days, keep your alarm set for 60 minutes earlier to start waking up when you *want* to, instead of when you *have* to. It's time to start launching each day with a *Miracle Morning* so that you can become the person you need to be to take yourself, your team, and your success to extraordinary levels.

What will you do with that hour? We're going to find out in the next chapter, but for now, simply continue reading this book during your *Miracle Morning* until you learn the whole routine.

Step Two: Join The Miracle Morning Community at www. MyTMMCommunity.com to connect with and get additional support from more than 15,000 like-minded early risers, many of whom have been generating extraordinary results with *The Miracle Morning* for years.

Step Three: Find a Miracle Morning accountability partner. Enroll someone—a friend, family member, or team member—to join you on this adventure and hold each other accountable to follow through until your Miracle Morning has become a lifelong habit.

TOP ONE PERCENT NETWORKER INTERVIEW

Jordan Adler

www.BeachMoney.com

Facebook.com/beachmoneyclub

Facebook.com/jordan.dreamon

Periscope: @JordanAdler

Twitter.com/jordanadler

A few of Jordan's accomplishments:

- Amazon Best Seller, Beach Money (100% of profits go to www.kiva.org)

- Newly Licensed Helicopter Pilot

- $20 million earned in Network Marketing

- 150,000 Distributors in 5 countries

- Will be the first Network Marketer in space (Scheduled to be one of the first civilian astronauts in history)

- Didn't make my first dime in network marketing until my 11th year of trying.

Jordan's Miracle Morning & Daily Rituals:

- Built my life around travel and lifestyle. No real morning routine however I split my time between 2 mountain residences (one in a ghost town and one in the forest) and a number of beach properties owned in a partnership.

- Coffee on the deck in the forest or at a beach cafe depending on where I am - completely unplugged - Just be present in the moment for at least 1 hour a day.

- Fly the helicopter at least once a week. Usually just around Las Vegas and the Red Rocks

- Read or listen to personal development daily 20-30 minutes

- Exercise with hot yoga or fitness training at least 3 times a week in the morning.

- Emails are usually done once or twice a week late at night but rarely in the morning. Email tends to take me off task and so I avoid getting sucked in. I schedule my email time so it doesn't become all-consuming.

- I keep a to-do list and check things off throughout the day as I accomplish them.

- I schedule my productive business building activities first (Business Presentations, Follow Up, Conference Calls, Training) and then work everything else in around this. Business Building Activities always take top priority.

- I schedule my personal time so that business doesn't encroach on it. As an entrepreneur, it's too easy to let work become all consuming. I take 2 vacations per month.

BONUS INTERVIEW FOR *MIRACLE MORNING FOR NETWORK MARKETING* READERS

Each of the Top One Percent Networkers that are featured in this book were interviewed by Pat Petrini about not only their morning routines, but their tips, techniques and strategies that have been critical in helping them become the best of the best in network marketing.

For your free and exclusive interview with Jordan, go to
www.TMMforNetworkMarketers.com/Adler

TOP ONE PERCENT NETWORKER INTERVIEW

Todd Falcone

www.ToddFalcone.com

Facebook.com/toddfalconefan

Twitter.com/todd_falcone

Periscope: @Todd_Falcone

Todd has developed organizations in the tens of thousands in five different companies during the 20-year span of his active career as a distributor in the field. Todd now invests all of his time teaching and training the exact same strategies and principles that led him to success.

He has presented to hundreds of audiences both domestically and abroad, including regional, national and international corporate conventions, local events hosted by leading distributors, conference calls, webinars, as well as his own live trainings conducted throughout the year.

Todd's Miracle Morning & Daily Rituals:

- Early AM: Gym or Hike while listening to business podcasts
- Home shower. Straight upstairs to office.
- Check emails, social media, etc
- Most days are 8 to 4 focused on talking to leaders, writing and producing content.
- Family break.
- Conference calls.
- Kids to bed.
- Back upstairs to office...learning something new, looking at calendar for tomorrow am

BONUS INTERVIEW FOR *MIRACLE MORNING FOR NETWORK MARKETING* READERS

Each of the Top One Percent Networkers that are featured in this book were interviewed by Pat Petrini about not only their morning routines, but their tips, techniques and strategies that have been critical in helping them become the best of the best in network marketing.

For your free and exclusive interview with Todd, go to www. TMMforNetworkMarketers.com/Todd

— 3 —
THE LIFE S.A.V.E.R.S.
SIX PRACTICES GUARANTEED TO SAVE YOU
FROM A LIFE OF UNFULFILLED POTENTIAL

"What Hal has done with his acronym S.A.V.E.R.S. is taken the best practices—developed over centuries of human consciousness development—and condensed the best of the best into a daily morning ritual. A ritual that is now part of my day. Many people do one of the SAVERS daily. For example, many people do the E, they exercise every morning. Others do S for silence or meditation, or S for scribing or journaling. But until Hal packaged SAVERS, no one was doing all six ancient best practices every morning. The Miracle Morning is perfect for very busy, successful people. Going through SAVERS every morning is like pumping rocket fuel into my body, mind, and spirit... before I start my day, every day."

—ROBERT KIYOSAKI, best-selling author,
Rich Dad, Poor Dad

When Hal experienced the second of his two self-proclaimed rock bottoms, both of which you can read about in *The Miracle Morning*, he began his own quest for the fastest way to take his personal development to the next level. So, he went in search of the daily practices of the world's most successful people.

After discovering six of the most proven, timeless personal development practices, Hal first attempted to determine which one or two would accelerate his success the fastest. Then he asked himself, *What would happen if I did ALL of them?*

Hal and I have been friends for well over a decade, and I saw firsthand his total transformation after discovering, implementing, and mastering those practices, which he came to call the Life S.A.V.E.R.S.

To my astonishment, Hal changed almost overnight. But it wasn't just him. I watched countless others adopt the Life S.A.V.E.R.S. and transform themselves, too. And I soon followed.

Why the Life S.A.V.E.R.S. Work

The Life S.A.V.E.R.S. are simple but profoundly effective daily morning practices that help you plan and live your life on your terms. They're designed to start your day in a peak physical, mental, emotional, and spiritual state so that you both continually improve and will ALWAYS perform at your best.

I know, I know. You don't have time. You probably feel like you can barely squeeze in what you have to do already, never mind what you want to. But I "didn't have time" either. And yet, here I am with more time, and more prosperity, than I've ever had.

In a few chapters, we're going to take a serious look at how much time you *really* have with something called "The Wealth Formula." I think you might be surprised!

What you need to realize right now is that your Miracle Morning will create time for you. The Life S.A.V.E.R.S. are the vehicle to help you stop working harder and longer and begin working smarter and more efficiently instead. The practices help you build energy, see priorities more clearly, and help you find the stress-free productive flow in your life.

In other words, the Life S.A.V.E.R.S. don't take more time from your day but ultimately add more to it.

Each letter in S.A.V.E.R.S. represents one of the best practices of the most successful network marketers on the planet. And they're also the same activities that bring new levels of peace, clarity, motivation, and energy to your life. They are:

Silence

Affirmations

Visualization

Exercise

Reading

Scribing

These practices are the best possible use of your newfound morning time. They're customizable to fit you, your life, and your goals. And you can start first thing tomorrow morning.

Let's go through each of the six practices in detail.

S is for Silence

Silence, the first practice of the Life S.A.V.E.R.S., is a key habit for network marketers. If you're surrounded by the endless barrage of phone calls, emails, presentations, opportunity meetings, cold calls, tracking sheets, and new product launches that make up a life in network marketing, this is your opportunity to STOP and BREATHE!

Most people start the day by checking email, texts, and group volume numbers on their smart phones. And most people struggle to build their businesses. It's not a coincidence. Starting each day with a period of silence instead will immediately reduce your stress levels and help you begin the day with the kind of calm and clarity that you need in order to focus on what's most important.

Many of the most successful people in network marketing, but also in all professions, are daily practitioners of silence. It's not surprising that Oprah practices stillness—or that she does nearly all of the other Life S.A.V.E.R.S., too. Musicians Katy Perry and Russell Brand practice transcendental meditation, as do Sheryl Crow and Sir Paul McCartney. Film and television stars Jennifer Aniston, Ellen Degeneres, Jerry Seinfeld, Howard Stern, Cameron Diaz, Clint Eastwood, and Hugh Jackman have all spoken of their daily meditation practice. Even famous billionaires Ray Dalio and Rupert Murdoch have attributed their *financial* success to practicing stillness on a daily basis. You'll be in good (and quiet) company by doing the same.

If it seems like I'm asking you to simply do nothing, let me clarify: you have a number of choices for how to build your practice of silence. In no particular order, here are a few to get you started:

- Meditation
- Prayer
- Reflection
- Deep breathing
- Gratitude

Whichever you choose, be sure you don't stay in bed for your period of silence, and better still, get out of your bedroom altogether.

The Benefits of Silence

How many times as network marketers do we find ourselves in stressful situations? How many times are we dealing with immediate obstacles that take us away from our vision or plan? No, those aren't trick questions—the answer is the same for both: every single day. Stress is one of the most common reasons that network marketers lose focus and lose business. Daily, I face the ever-present distractions of other people encroaching on my schedule and the inevitable fires I must extinguish. Quieting the mind allows me to put those things aside and focus on working *on* my business instead of *in* it.

But the effect goes beyond productivity. Excessive stress is terrible for your health, too. It triggers your fight or flight response, and that releases a cascade of toxic hormones that can stay in your body for days. That's fine if you experience that type of stress only occasionally. But when the constant barrage of a life in network marketing keeps the adrenaline flowing all the time, the negative impact on your health adds up.

Silence in the form of meditation, however, can reduce stress, and as a result, improve your health. A major study run by several groups, including the National Institutes of Health, the American Medical Association, the Mayo Clinic, and scientists from both Harvard and Stanford, stated that meditation can reduce stress and high blood pressure. A recent study by Dr. Norman Rosenthal, a world-renowned psychiatrist who works with the David Lynch Foundation, even found that people who practice meditation are 30 percent less likely to die from heart disease.

Another study from Harvard found that just eight weeks of meditation could lead to "increased grey-matter density in the hippocampus, known to be important for learning and memory, and in structures associated with self-awareness, compassion and introspection."

Practicing silence, in other words, can help you reduce your stress, improve cognitive performance, and replace medication with meditation at the same time.

Guided Meditations and Meditation Apps

Meditation is like anything else—if you've never done it before, then it can be difficult or feel awkward at first. If you are a first time meditator, I recommend starting with a guided meditation.

Here are a few of my favorite meditation apps that are available for both iPhone/iPad and Android devices:

- Headspace
- Calm
- Omvana
- Simply Being

There are both subtle and significant differences among these meditation apps, one of which is the voice of the person speaking.

If you don't have a device that allows you to download apps, simply go to YouTube or Google and search on the keywords "Guided Meditation."

Another really cool tool that I've been using lately is called Holosync. It costs around $150 for the program, however, I was blown away at the immediate difference in the depth of my meditation sessions when I started using it. If you want to check it out, just go to www.TMMforNetworkMarketers.com/holosync.

Miracle Morning (Individual) Meditation

When you're ready to try an unguided meditation, here is a simple, step-by-step meditation you can use during your Miracle Morning, even if you've never meditated before.

- Before beginning your meditation, it's important to prepare your mindset and set your expectations. This is a time for you to quiet your mind and let go of the compulsive need to constantly be thinking about something—reliving the past or worrying about the future, but never living fully in the present. This is the time to let go of your stresses, take a break from worrying about your problems, and be fully present in this moment. It is a time to access the essence of who you truly are— to go deeper than what you have, what you do, or the labels you've accepted as who you are. If this sounds foreign to you, or too new age, that's okay. I've felt the same way. It's probably only because you've never tried it before. But thankfully, you're about to.

- Find a quiet, comfortable place to sit. You can sit up straight on the couch, on a chair, on the floor, or on a pillow for added comfort.

- Sit upright, cross-legged. You can close your eyes, or you can look down at a point on the ground about two feet in front of you.

- Begin by focusing on your breath, taking slow, deep breaths. Breathe in through the nose and out through the mouth. The most effective breathing causes your belly to expand and not your chest.

- Now start pacing your breath; breathe in slowly for a count of three seconds (one one thousand, two one thousand, three one thousand), hold it in for another three counts, and then breathe out slowly for a final count of three. Feel your thoughts and emotions settling down as you focus on your breath. Be aware that, as you attempt to quiet your mind, thoughts will still come in to pay a visit. Simply acknowledge them, and then let them go, always returning your focus to your breath.

- Try being fully present in this moment. This is often referred to as just being. Not thinking, not doing, just being. Continue to follow your breath, and imagine inhaling positive, loving and peaceful energy, and exhaling all of your worries and stress. Enjoy the quiet. Enjoy the moment. Just breathe … Just be.

- If you find that you have a constant influx of thoughts, it may be helpful for you to focus on a single word, phrase, or mantra and repeat it over and over again to yourself as you inhale and exhale. For example, you might try something like this: (On the inhale) "I inhale confidence …" (As you exhale) "I exhale fear …" You can swap the word confidence for whatever you feel you need to bring more of into your life (love, faith, energy, etc.), and swap the word fear with whatever you feel you need to let go of (stress, worry, resentment, etc.).

Meditation is a gift you can give yourself every day. My time spent meditating has become one of my favorite parts of the routine. It's a time to be at peace and to experience gratitude and freedom from my day-to-day stressors and worries.

Think of daily meditation as a temporary vacation from your problems. While your problems will still be there when you finish your daily meditation, you'll find that you're much more centered and better equipped to solve them.

A is for Affirmations

Have you ever wondered why some of the top network marketers around you regularly surpass even your best month in business?

Or why others in the same business can only produce enough to barely scrape by? Time and time again, it is a network marketer's *mindset* that shows up as the driving factor in their performance.

From prospective clients to colleagues, those around you can sense your mindset. It shows up undeniably in your language, your confidence, and your demeanor. And as a result, your attitude affects the entire business building process, from opening conversations to enrolling a new business builder. Show me a great network marketer, and I'll show you someone with a great mindset.

I know firsthand, though, how difficult it can be for network marketers (a.k.a. *marketers*) to maintain confidence and enthusiasm—not to mention motivation—during the rollercoaster ride of building their businesses. Mindset is largely something we adopt without conscious thought—at a subconscious level, we have all been programmed to think, believe, act, and talk to ourselves a certain way. When times get tough, we revert to our habitual, programmed mindset.

Our programming has come from many influences, including what we've have been told by others, what we've told ourselves, and all of our good and bad life experiences. That programming expresses itself throughout our lives, including in our businesses. And that means if we want a better business, we need better mental programming.

Affirmations are a tool for doing just that. By repeatedly telling yourself who you want to be, what you want to accomplish, and how you are going to accomplish it, your subconscious mind will shift your beliefs and behavior. You'll automatically believe and act in new ways, and eventually manifest your affirmations into your reality.

Science has proven that affirmations—when done correctly—are one of the most effective tools for quickly becoming the person you need to be to achieve everything you want in your life. And yet, affirmations also have a bad rap. Many have tried them only to be disappointed, with little or no results.

Why the Old Way of Doing Affirmations Doesn't Work

For decades, countless so-called experts and gurus have taught affirmations in ways that have proven to be ineffective and set people up for failure, time and time again. Here are two of the most common problems with affirmations.

Lying to Yourself Doesn't Work

I am a millionaire. No, you're not.

I have 7% body fat. No, you don't.

I have achieved all of my goals this year. Nope. Sorry, you haven't.

This method of creating affirmations that are written as if you've already become or achieved something may be the single biggest reason that affirmations haven't worked for most people.

With this technique, every time you recite an affirmation that simply isn't rooted in truth, your subconscious will resist it. As an intelligent human being who isn't delusional, lying to yourself repeatedly will never be the optimum strategy. *The truth will always prevail.*

Passive Language Doesn't Produce Results

Many affirmations have been designed to make you feel good by creating an empty promise of something you desire. For example, here is a popular money affirmation that's been perpetuated for decades, by many world-famous gurus:

I am a money magnet. Money flows to me effortlessly and in abundance.

This type of affirmation might make you feel good in the moment by giving you a false sense of relief from your financial worries, but it won't generate any income. People who sit back and wait for money to magically show up are cash poor.

To generate financial abundance (or any result you desire, for that matter), you've got to actually do something. Your actions must be in alignment with your desired results, and your affirmations must articulate and affirm both.

4 Steps to Create Affirmations That Increase Sales

Here are simple steps for creating and implementing results-oriented *Miracle Morning* affirmations, which will program both your conscious and subconscious mind to produce results and take your levels of personal and professional success beyond what you've ever experienced before.

Step 1: The Extraordinary Result You Are Committed to and Why

Notice I'm not starting with "What you want." Everyone wants things, but we don't get what we want; we get what we're committed to. You want to be a millionaire? Who cares; join that nonexclusive club. Oh wait, you're 100 percent committed to becoming a millionaire by clarifying and executing the necessary actions until the result is achieved? Okay, now we're talking.

Action: Start by writing down a (specific) extraordinary result or outcome—one that challenges you and would significantly improve your life and one that you are ready to commit to creating (even if you're not yet sure how you will do it). Then, reinforce your commitment by including your WHY, the compelling benefits that you'll get to experience.

Examples: *I am committed to doubling my income in the next 12 months, from $_____ to $_____, so that I can provide financial security for my family.*

Or…

I am 100 percent committed to losing _____ pounds and weighing _____ pounds by _____ (date) so that I have more energy and set an example of health and fitness for my kids.

Step 2: The Necessary Actions You Are Committed to Taking and When

Writing an affirmation that merely affirms what you *want* without affirming what you are committed to *doing* is one step above pointless and can actually be counter-productive by tricking your subconscious mind into thinking that the result will happen automatically, without effort.

Action: Clarify the (specific) action, activity, or habit that is required for you to achieve your ideal outcome, and clearly state WHEN and how often you will execute the necessary action.

Examples: *To guarantee that I double my income, I am committed to doubling my daily prospecting calls from 20 to 40 calls five days a week from 8:00 a.m. to 9:00 a.m.—NO MATTER WHAT.*

Or ...

To ensure that I lose _____ pounds, I am 100 percent committed to going to the gym 5 days per week and running on the treadmill for a minimum of 20 minutes each day from 6:00 a.m. to 7:00 a.m.

The more specific your actions are, the better. Be sure to include *frequency* (how often), *quantity* (how many), and *precise time frames* (which times you will begin and end your activities).

Step 3: Recite Your Affirmations Every Morning with Emotion

Remember, your *Miracle Morning* affirmations aren't designed merely to make you *feel good*. These are written statements that are strategically engineered to program your subconscious mind with the beliefs and overall mindset you need to achieve your desired outcomes, while directing your conscious mind to keep you focused on your highest priorities and taking the actions that will get you there.

However, in order for your affirmations to be effective, it is important that you tap into your emotions while reciting them. Mindlessly repeating an affirmation over and over again, without intentionally feeling its truth, will have minimal impact for you. You must take responsibility for generating authentic emotions, such as excitement and determination, and powerfully infusing those emotions into every affirmation you recite.

Action: Schedule time each day to read your affirmations in the morning (ideally during your Miracle Morning), to both program your subconscious and focus your conscious mind on what's most important to you and what you are committed to doing to make it your reality. That's right, you must read them daily. Reading an occasional affirmation is as effective as getting an occasional workout. You'll start seeing results only once you've made them a part of your daily routine.

Step 4: Constantly Update and Evolve Your Affirmations

As you continue to grow, improve, and evolve, so should your affirmations. When you come up with a new goal, dream, or any extraordinary result that you want to create for your life, add it to your affirmations.

Personally, I have affirmations for every single significant area of my life (finances, health, happiness, relationships, parenting, etc.) and am constantly updating my affirmations as I learn more. And I am always on the lookout for quotes, strategies, and philosophies that I can add to improve my mindset. Any time you come across an empowering quote or philosophy and think to yourself, *Man, that is a huge area of improvement for me*, add it to your affirmations.

Your programming can be changed and improved at any time, starting right now. You can reprogram any perceived limitations with new beliefs and behaviors so you can become as successful as you want to be, in any area of life you choose.

In summary, your new affirmations will articulate which extraordinary results you are committed to creating, why they are critically important to you, and most importantly, which necessary actions you are committed to taking, and precisely when you are committed to taking them to ensure that you attain and sustain the extraordinary levels of success that you truly want (and deserve) for your life.

Affirmations to Become a Top Network Marketer

In addition to the formula to create your affirmations, I have included this list of sample affirmations, which are regularly used by top network marketers to increase growth and productivity and to improve in different areas of their business. Feel free to include any of these that resonate with you.

- I leave every person I speak to better than I found them because I genuinely care about what is happening in their lives and I'm

What Do You Visualize?

Most network marketers are limited by visions of their past results, replaying previous failures and heartbreaks. Creative visualization, on the other hand, enables you to design the vision that will occupy your mind, ensuring that the greatest pull on you is your future—a compelling, exciting, and limitless future.

After I've read my affirmations, I sit upright, close my eyes, and take a few slow, deep breaths. For the next five to ten minutes, I simply visualize the *specific actions* that are necessary for my long- and short-term goals to become a reality.

Notice that I did *not* say that I visualize the results. Many people will disagree on this issue, but there are some studies that show that visualizing the victory (for example, standing on stage, the car, the house, the new team member, etc.) can actually diminish your drive because your brain has already experienced the reward on some level. Instead, I would recommend using visualization as a practice session for improving the skills or aspects of your life that you are working on. Visualize actions, not results.

In network marketing, you might picture yourself having fun and light conversations with prospects during morning phone calls. Spend time imagining your presentation with your prospect. What does it look like? How does it feel as you develop a great relationship? Picture yourself responding to objections and questions. You can really pick anything that is a critical action step or skill that you may not be performing at your best yet. Envisioning success will prepare you for, and almost ensure, a successful day.

3 Simple Steps for Miracle Morning Visualization

Directly after reading your affirmations is the perfect time to visualize yourself living in alignment with them.

Step 1: Get Ready

Some people like to play instrumental music in the background, such as classical or baroque (check out anything from the composer J.S. Bach), during their visualization. If you'd like to experiment with playing music, put it on with the volume relatively low. Personally, I find anything with words to be a distraction.

Now, sit up tall in a comfortable position. This can be on a chair, the couch, or the floor. Breathe deeply. Close your eyes, clear your mind, and get ready to visualize.

Step 2: Visualize What You Really Want

The greatest gift you can give to the people you love is to live up to your full potential. What does that look like for you? What do you really want? Forget about logic, limits, and being practical. If you could have anything you wanted, do anything you wanted, and be anything you wanted, what would you choose? What *specific actions* would you have to *do* to get it? What would you have to become? How would you act in different situations?

See, feel, hear, touch, taste, and smell every detail of your vision. Involve all of your senses to maximize the effectiveness of your visualization. The more vivid you make your vision, the more compelled you'll be to take the necessary actions to make it a reality.

Step 3: Visualize Who You Need To Be and What You Need To Do

Once you've created a clear mental picture of what you want, begin to visualize yourself living in total alignment with the person you need to be to achieve your vision. See yourself engaged in the positive actions you'll need to do each day (exercising, studying, working, writing, making calls, sending emails, etc.) and make sure you see yourself enjoying the process. See yourself smiling as you're running on that treadmill, filled with a sense of pride for your self-discipline to follow through.

Picture the look of determination on your face as you confidently, persistently make those phone calls, work on that report, or finally take action and make progress on that project you've been putting off for far too long. Visualize your co-workers, customers, family, friends, and spouse responding to your positive demeanor and optimistic outlook.

Final Thoughts on Visualization

When you combine reading your affirmations every morning with daily visualization, you will turbocharge the programming of your subconscious mind for success. You will begin to live in alignment with your ideal vision and make it a reality. When you visualize daily, you align your thoughts and feelings with your vision. This makes it easier to maintain the motivation you need to continue taking the necessary actions. Visualization can be a powerful aid in overcoming self-limiting habits, such as procrastination, and in taking the actions necessary to achieve your goals.

E is for Exercise

Exercise should be a staple of your Miracle Morning. Even a few minutes of exercise each morning significantly enhances your health, improves your self-confidence and emotional well being, and enables you to think better and concentrate longer. You'll also notice how quickly your energy level increases with daily exercise, and your clients will notice it, too—even over the phone.

Personal development experts and self-made multi-millionaire entrepreneurs Eben Pagan and Anthony Robbins (who is also a bestselling author) both agree that the number one key to success is to "start every morning off with a personal success ritual." Included in both of their success rituals is some type of morning exercise. If it's good enough for Eben and Tony, it's good enough for me.

Lest you think you have to engage in triathlon or marathon training, think again. Your morning exercise also doesn't need to replace an afternoon or evening regimen, if you already have one in place. You can still hit the gym after you've made prospecting calls or done a few product demonstrations. However, the benefits from adding as little as five minutes of morning exercise are undeniable, including improved blood pressure and blood sugar levels and decreased risk of all kinds of scary things like heart disease, osteoporosis, cancer, and diabetes. Maybe most importantly, a little exercise in the morning will increase your energy levels for the rest of the day.

You can go for a walk or run, hit the gym, throw on a P90X or Insanity DVD, watch a yoga video on YouTube, or find a Life S.A.V.E.R.S. buddy to play some early morning racquetball. There's also an excellent app called 7 Minute Workout that gives you a full body workout in—you guessed it—seven minutes. The choice is yours—just pick one and do it.

As a network marketer, you are on the go. You need an endless reserve of energy to capitalize on all of the opportunities coming your way, and a daily morning exercise practice is going to provide it.

Exercise for Your Brain

Even if you don't care about your physical health, consider that exercise is simply going to make you smarter, and that can only help your business acumen. Dr. Steven Masley, a Florida physician and nutritionist with a health practice geared toward executives, explains how exercise creates a direct connection to your cognitive ability.

"If we're talking about brain performance, the best predictor of brain speed is aerobic capacity—how well you can run up a hill is very strongly correlated with brain speed and cognitive shifting ability," Masley said.

Masley has designed a corporate wellness program based on the work he's done with more than 1,000 patients. "The average person going into these programs will increase brain speed by 25–30 percent."

Imagine how a 25–30 percent increase in brain speed could increase your ability to respond to your business builders and customers in a positive way and offer helpful solutions. How much could you increase your business just by having more effective and efficient conversations with prospects? Picture yourself getting on the phone with clients or prospective team members after a workout. What would your state of mind be? How different would you feel? What would the people you're talking to gain from these conversations? What might that do for your business?

Hal chose yoga and began practicing it shortly after he created the Miracle Morning. He's been doing it and loving it ever since. My exercise routine is usually a run around my neighborhood while listening to great podcasts or audiobooks followed by three sets of push-ups, sit-ups, and handstand push-ups. For me, this accomplishes several things at once: the run helps to wake me up and get my Miracle Morning started, I get a dose of vitamin D for my mind and body, I get a combination of cardio and muscular workout, *and* I get a dose of inspiration from whatever I may be listening to.

My wife and I also keep a pull-up bar in the doorway to our bedroom, and neither of us are allowed to walk through it anytime during the day without doing at least a few pull-ups. That ends up being quite a few pull-ups everyday! I enjoy the variety. Find what resonates with you, and make it a part of your Miracle Morning.

Final Thoughts on Exercise

You know that, if you want to maintain good health and increase your energy, you must exercise consistently. That's not news to anyone. But what also isn't news is how easy it is to make excuses. Two of the biggest are "I don't have time" and "I'm too tired." And those are just the first two on the list. There is no limit to the excuses that you can think of. And the more creative you are, the more excuses you can come up with!

That's the beauty of incorporating exercise into your Miracle Morning—it happens before your day wears you out, and before you have an entire day to come up with new excuses. Because it happens first, the Miracle Morning is a surefire way to avoid all of those excuses, and to make exercise a daily habit.

Legal disclaimer: Hopefully this goes without saying, but you should consult your doctor or physician before beginning any exercise regimen, especially if you are experiencing any physical pain, discomfort, disabilities, etc. You may need to modify or even refrain from your exercise routine to meet your individual needs.

R is for Reading

One of the fastest ways to achieve everything you want is to model successful people. For every goal you have, there's a good chance there's an expert out there who has already achieved the same thing, or something similar. As Tony Robbins says, "Success leaves clues."

Fortunately, some of the best of the best have shared their stories throughout history in the form of writing. And that means all those success blueprints are just waiting out there for anyone willing to invest some time in reading. Books are a limitless supply of help and mentorship, right at your fingertips.

Occasionally, I'll hear somebody say "I'm just not a big reader." I get it. I used to have that attitude as well. I always think back to what my mentor used to say: "The greatest minds of our time and in human history have spent years, and sometimes decades, to condense the best of what they know into a few pages that can be read in a few hours and purchased for a few dollars … but you're not a big reader. That's a bad decision." Ouch!

Want to be a multi-millionaire network marketer? Looking to build better relationships in your life? Do you want to improve your leadership skills? Hoping to take your financial knowledge to a level ten? Be a reader!

Here are some of my favorites that will specifically help you in the areas of network marketing, sales and personal growth. These are not good books. These are *great* books that will significantly impact you if you let them:

On Network Marketing & Selling:

- *Go Pro—7 Steps to Becoming a Network Marketing Professional* by Eric Worre
- *Your First Year in Network Marketing: Overcome Your Fears, Experience Success, and Achieve Your Dreams* by Mark Yarnell
- *The 10X Rule: The Only Difference Between Success and Failure* by Grant Cardone

- *Magnetic Sponsoring: How to Attract Endless New Leads and Distributors to You Automatically* by Mike Dillard
- *Questions are the Answers* by Allan Pease
- *The Greatest Salesman in the World* by Og Mandino
- *The SPEED of Trust: The One Thing That Changes Everything* by Stephen M.R. Covey
- *How To Master The Art Of Selling* by Tom Hopkins

On Mindset:

- *The Art of Exceptional Living* by Jim Rohn
- *The One Thing: The Surprisingly Simple Truth Behind Extraordinary Results* by Gary Keller and Jay Papasan
- *The Seven Habits of Highly Effective People: Powerful Lessons in Personal Change* by Stephen M.R. Covey
- *Mastery* by Robert Greene
- *The 4 Hour Workweek: Escape 9-5, Live Anywhere, and Join the New Rich* by Tim Ferriss
- *The Game of Life and How to Play It* by Florence Scovel Shinn
- *The Compound Effect* by Darren Hardy
- *Taking Life Head On: How to Love the Life You Have While You Create the Life of Your Dreams* by Hal Elrod
- *Think and Grow Rich* by Napoleon Hill
- *Vision to Reality: How Short Term Massive Action Equals Long Term Maximum Results* by Honorée Corder

In addition to finding network marketing success, you can transform your relationships, increase your self-confidence, improve your communication or persuasion skills, learn how to become healthy, and improve any other area of your life you can think of. Head to your local bookstore—or do what I do and head to Amazon.com—and you'll find more books than you can possibly imagine on any area of your life you want to improve.

For a complete list of our favorite personal development books—including those that have made the biggest impact on our success and happiness—check out the Recommended Reading list at TMMBook.com.

How Much Should You Read?

I recommend making a commitment to read a minimum of ten pages per day (although five is okay to start with if you read slowly or don't yet enjoy reading).

Ten pages does not seem like much, but let's do the math. Reading ten pages a day gives you 3,650 pages a year. That stacks up to approximately eighteen 200-page personal development or self-improvement books! And, all in 10–15 minutes of reading, or 15–30 minutes if you read more slowly.

Let me ask you, if you read 18 personal development or success books in the next year, do you think you'll be more knowledgeable, capable, and confident? Do you think you'll be a better you? Absolutely! Reading 10 pages per day is not going to break you, but it will sure make you.

Final Thoughts on Reading

Begin with the end in mind—what do you hope to gain from the book? Take a moment to do this now by asking yourself what you want to gain from reading this one.

- Books don't have to be read cover to cover, nor do they have to be finished. Remember that this is *your* reading time. Be sure to use the table of contents of a book to make sure that you are reading the parts that you care about most, and don't hesitate to put it down and move to another if you aren't enjoying it. There is too much incredible information out there to spend any time on the mediocre.

- Many Miracle Morning practitioners use their reading time to catch up on their religious texts, such as the Bible or Torah.

- Feel free to underline, circle, highlight, dog-ear, and take notes in the margins of this book. The process of marking books as you read allows you to come back at any time and recapture all of the key lessons, ideas, and benefits without needing to read the book again, cover to cover. If you read on a digital reader, such as Kindle, Nook, or via iBooks, notes and highlighting are easily organized, so you can see them each time you flip through the book, or you can go directly to a list of your notes and highlights.

- Summarize key ideas, insights and memorable passages in your journal. You can build your own brief summary of your favorite books so you can revisit the key content any time in just minutes.

- Rereading good personal development books is an underutilized yet very effective strategy. Rarely can you read a book once and internalize all of the value. Achieving mastery in any area requires repetition. I've read books like *Think and Grow Rich* as many as three times and often refer back to them throughout the year. Why not try it out with this book? Commit to rereading it as soon as you're finished, to deepen your learning and give yourself more time to master your Miracle Morning.

- Take advantage of action steps and action plans set out in the books you read. While reading is a great way to learn new strategies, it is the implantation and practice of these new strategies that will really improve your life and business. Are you committed to implementing what you're learning in this book by taking action and following through with at least one of the 30-Day Challenges at the end of each chapter?

S is for Scribing

Scribing is simply another word for writing. I write in my journal for five to ten minutes during my Miracle Morning, usually during reading time, and then during an additional period of contemplation. By getting your thoughts out of your head and putting them in writing, you gain valuable insights you'd otherwise never see.

The Scribing element of your Miracle Morning enables you to document your insights, ideas, breakthroughs, realizations, successes, and lessons learned, as well as any areas of opportunity, personal growth, or improvement. Use your journal to note your network marketing strengths, what went right in each day's sales calls and opportunity and product presentations, and add any distinctions you want to remember later and perhaps work on.

If you're like Hal, you probably have at least a few half-used and barely touched journals and notebooks. It wasn't until he started his own Miracle Morning practice that it quickly became a favored habit. As Tony Robbins has said many times, "A life worth living is a life worth recording."

Writing will give you the daily benefits of consciously directing your thoughts, but what's even more powerful are the insights you'll gain from reviewing your journals, from cover to cover, afterwards—especially at the end of the year.

It is hard to put into words how overwhelmingly constructive the experience of going back and reviewing your journals can be. *The Miracle Morning for Real Estate Agents* co-author, Michael Maher, is an avid practitioner of the Life S.A.V.E.R.S. Part of Michael's morning routine is to write down his appreciations and affirmations in what he calls his Blessings Book. Michael says it best:

"What you appreciate … APPRECIATES. It was time to take my insatiable appetite for what I wanted and replace it with an insatiable appetite and gratitude for what I do have. Write your appreciations, be grateful and appreciative, and you will have more of those things you crave—better relationships, more material goods, more happiness."

There is strength in writing down what you appreciate, and reviewing this material can change your mindset on a challenging day.

While there are many worthwhile benefits of keeping a daily journal, here are a few more of my favorites. With daily scribing, you'll

- Gain Clarity—Journaling will give you more clarity and understanding and allow you to brainstorm, as well as help you work through problems.

- Capture Ideas—You will capture and be able to expand on

your ideas, and journaling also prevents you from losing the important ones you are saving for an opportune moment in the future.

- Review Lessons—Journaling provides a place to reference and review all of the lessons you've learned.

Acknowledge Your Progress—It's wonderful to go back and re-read your journal entries from a year ago and see how much progress you've made. It's one of the most empowering, confidence-inspiring, and enjoyable experiences. It can't be duplicated any other way.

Effective Journaling

Here are three simple steps to get started with journaling or improve your current journaling process.

1. Choose a Format: Physical or Digital. You'll want to decide up front if you want to go with a traditional, physical journal or a digital journal (such as on your computer or an app for your phone or tablet). If you aren't sure, just experiment with both and see which you prefer.

2. Get a Journal. Almost anything can work, but when it comes to a physical journal, there is something to be said for an attractive, durable journal that you enjoy looking at—after all, ideally you're going to have it for the rest of your life. I recommend getting a journal that is not only lined, but also dated, with room to write for all 365 days of the year. I've found that having a pre-designated (dated) space to write keeps you accountable to follow through each day since you can't help but notice when you miss a day or two.

Here are a few of my favorite physical journals:

- *The Miracle Morning Companion Planner* is your hands-on guide for building a happier and more fulfilling life and career. This 12-month, undated planner allows you to start at any time of the year! Incorporating and tracking the Life S.A.V.E.R.S. each day will help you to be more present and intentional in each moment, own every aspect of your day, and to get the most out of your life. Check out a free preview here: MiracleMorning.com/PlannerSample.

- *Five Minute Journal* (FiveMinuteJournal.com) has become very popular among top performers. It has a very specific format for each day, giving you prompts, such as "I am grateful for …" and "What would make today great?" It takes five minutes or less, and includes an Evening option, which allows you to review your day.

- *The Miracle Morning Journal* (available on Amazon or at MiracleMorningJournal.com) is designed specifically to enhance and support your Miracle Morning and to keep you organized and accountable and to track your Life S.A.V.E.R.S. each day. You can also download a free sample of *The Miracle Morning Journal* today at TMMbook.com to make sure it's right for you.

- BulletJournal.com. It's a journal you buy, or it's a journal system you incorporate into the journal of your choosing. You get to choose; either way, it's great!

If you prefer to use a digital journal, there are also many choices available. Here are a few of my favorites:

- Five Minute Journal (FiveMinuteJournal.com) also offers an iPhone app, which follows the same format as the physical version and also sends you helpful reminders to input your entries each morning and evening. It also allows you to upload photos to create visual memories.

- Day One (DayOneApp.com) is a popular journaling app, and it's perfect if you don't want any structure or any limits on how much you can write. Day One offers a blank page, so if you like to write lengthy journal entries, this may be the app for you.

- Penzu (Penzu.com) is a popular online journal, which doesn't require an iPhone, iPad, or Android device. All you need is a computer.

Again, it really comes down to your preference and the features you want. Type "online journal" into Google or "journal" into the app store, and you'll get a variety of choices.

Customizing the Life S.A.V.E.R.S.

I want to share a few ideas specifically geared toward customizing the Life S.A.V.E.R.S. based on your schedule and preferences. Your current morning routine might allow you to fit in only a 6-, 20-, or 30-minute Miracle Morning, or you might choose to do a longer version on the weekends.

Here is an example of a fairly common 60-minute Miracle Morning schedule, using the Life S.A.V.E.R.S.

Silence: 10 minutes

Affirmations: 10 minutes

Visualization: 5 minutes

Exercise: 10 minutes

Reading: 20 minutes

Scribing: 5 minutes

You can customize the sequence, too. I prefer to do my exercise first as a way to increase my blood flow and wake myself up. However, you might prefer to do exercise as your last activity in the Life S.A.V.E.R.S. so you're not sweaty during your *Miracle Morning*. Hal prefers to start with a period of peaceful, purposeful silence so that he can wake up slowly, clear his mind, and focus his energy and intentions. However, this is your Miracle Morning, not mine—feel free to experiment with different sequences and see which you like best.

Final Thoughts on the Life S.A.V.E.R.S.

Everything is difficult before it's easy. Every new experience is uncomfortable before it's comfortable. The more you practice the Life S.A.V.E.R.S., the more natural and normal each of them will feel. Hal's first time meditating was almost his last because his mind raced like a Ferrari and his thoughts bounced around uncontrollably like the silver sphere in a pinball machine. Now, he loves meditation, and while he's still no master, he says he's decent at it.

Similarly, I had trouble with affirmations when I first started my Miracle Mornings. I didn't know what I wanted to affirm. So, I stole a few from *The Miracle Morning* and added a few that came to mind. It was okay, but they didn't really *mean* much to me initially. Over time, as I encountered things that struck me as powerful, I added them to my affirmations and adjusted the ones I had. Now, my affirmations mean a lot to me, and the daily act of using them is far more powerful.

I invite you to begin practicing the Life S.A.V.E.R.S. now, so you can become familiar and comfortable with each of them and get a jump-start before you begin The Miracle Morning 30-Day Life Transformation Challenge in chapter 2.

If your biggest concern is still finding time, don't worry; I've got you covered. You can actually do the entire Miracle Morning— receiving the full benefits of all six Life S.A.V.E.R.S. in only six minutes a day! Simply do each of the Life S.A.V.E.R.S. for one minute each: close your eyes and enjoy a moment of silence, visualize achieved single action that you want to mentally practice for the day, say your affirmations (or repeat your favorite affirmation over and over). You can then do jumping jacks or push-ups or crunches, then grab a book and read a paragraph, and then jot down a few thoughts in your journal. These six minutes will serve to set you on the right path for the day—and you can always devote more time later in the day when your schedule permits or the opportunity presents itself.

In the coming chapters, we are going to cover *a lot* of information that has the potential to turn you into a true network marketing professional, should you choose to apply it. And, one of the great things about building a passive income and working from home is that your Miracle Morning doesn't have the time constraints that it might if you have to leave for a job. Personally, my Miracle Morning has grown into a three hour monster that I absolutely love! If you'd like to check it out, just go to www.PatPetrini. com/MiracleMorning. On to the next chapter!

TOP ONE PERCENT NETWORKER INTERVIEW

Justin Prince

www.IAmJustinPrince.com

Facebook.com/justin.prince.90

YouTube.com/user/justinprince3

A few of Justin's accomplishments:

- Husband and father of 4 kids

- Built two multi-million dollar businesses in his 20s

- Earned his first million dollars in his 20s

- Became an equity partner in a $300M a year global business at age 32

- Helped create a Social Retail business model that led to the acquisition of well over 100,000 customers in under two years.

- Built an annual income that places him in the top 1% of income earners in his network marketing globally.

- He is a sought after speaker, consultant, entrepreneur and thought leader in leadership, sales and group motivation.

Justin's Miracle Morning & Daily Rituals:

- The first thing I do when I wake up is listen to between 5 to 20 minutes of positive information. Usually from YouTube and I have positive "thought of the day" messages both emailed and texted to me. I "guard" the first few minutes of my day. I want to "pour water into my well" because I know that I cannot give what I don't have. I want to make sure my "well" has more than enough water for me, my family and the people I will pour into that day. I usually begin listening to this as I use the restroom first thing in the morning. Maybe too many details but they asked to be specific ;-)

- I then brush and floss my teeth and splash my face with cold water. I have my headphones in listening to positive information as I get ready to go to the gym.

- Next I go downstairs and wake up my oldest son so that he can get ready to come with me to the gym. I go through my daughters and youngest sons rooms and give them quick kisses as they still sleep. These moments with each child are important to me. It helps me feel a connection to my kids.

- First thing in the morning I begin drinking a lot of water. I do this throughout my workout as well.

- I make my son some breakfast and depending on what workout plan I am on at the time make me some egg whites or I go to the gym "fasted" on an empty stomach.

- As we drive I have my son listen to one of the "thoughts of the day" that I listened to earlier and give me his feedback on what he feels like the point is or the message is. I love hearing his insights through the eyes of a child.

- When we get to the gym I make sure my son has his basketball workout routine. I have found that if he has a plan and a target to get through he is much more effective than if he just "shoots around."

- I start my workout for about the next 45 to 60 minutes. I go through different workout routines. I am always trying new programs or methodology that I read about. Regardless of the methodology I always do weight training. Even when I do cardio, weights are always part of my days. While working out is good for my physical health I feel that is key for my mental health.

- I will drop my son off and either shower and get ready at home or head to the office to shower. I almost always have a protein shake after my workouts. I will also eat oatmeal and egg whites as well. I have learned that a good protein meal sets me up to eat healthy the rest of the day.

- At night I do my best to tuck my kids in. My girls like to "snuggle" and for me to tell them stories. I also try and talk to them about their day and their lives. We take turn saying our prayers together and I tuck them in.

- I come upstairs and take time talking with my wife. After being with kids all day it is good for her to have a conversation with an adult and for us to catch up on the day and to hear how she is doing.

- We try and go to bed at the same time. Sometimes when we do I will spend that time with her but after our conversation go back to work.

- Once I am ready to shut it down I try and build an "unwind" time of about 20 to 30 minutes. During this time I will pray, plan my next day, listen to inspiring information or read good books.

- I put my phone in "sleep mode". I do this to try and avoid being distracted with texts, emails or messages that come in.

- My sleep is very important to me. I need sleep. I can go on a little sleep for a few days but for me to be sharp I need good sleep. Because of this, I will take "power naps" if I am lagging behind on my sleep. I can take a power nap for 10 minutes and recharge and refocus.

BONUS INTERVIEW FOR *MIRACLE MORNING FOR NETWORK MARKETING* READERS

Each of the Top One Percent Networkers that are featured in this book were interviewed by Pat Petrini about not only their morning routines, but their tips, techniques and strategies that have been critical in helping them become the best of the best in network marketing.

For your free and exclusive interview with Justin, go to www. TMMforNetworkMarketers.com/Justin

TOP ONE PERCENT NETWORKER INTERVIEW

Jessica Ellerman

www.JessicaEllerman.com

Facebook.com/jeveretteellerman

Jessica was a national champion gymnast and later became a hairdresser by trade for 8 years before being introduced to network marketing.

A few of Jessica's accomplishments:

- Car Earner

- Multiple Trip Earner

- Over 50 six figure earners that have been personally coached by her

- Earned the title "Inspirational Leader of the Year"

- #1 Recruiter in her company

- Top 5 earner in her company

- Featured in Success From Home Magazine

- Rated Top 10 Female Networker in 2015

- Paul Orberson Award recipient in 2015

Jessica's Miracle Morning & Daily Rituals:

- My day starts in bed. I have no alarm besides kids so I wake up when I'm done sleeping. One of my favorite perks of the industry is no alarm!

- I say my affirmations, meditate and bring the good energy into my being.

- Turn my phone on and answer texts, messages, and emails.

- Shower and get ready for the day, ALWAYS listening to music. Upbeat music.

- Go downstairs, grab coffee, supplements and make breakfast (5 eggs whites with spinach, 1/4 cup oats cooked with blueberries).

- Log into social media and check for updates, send texts, and post something positive on all my social media outlets.

- Check in with my leaders. Make sure everyone is supported and cast vision with them. Make any travel plans with them and add to schedules.

- Out the door for 5-7 meetings per day.

BONUS INTERVIEW FOR *MIRACLE MORNING FOR NETWORK MARKETING* READERS

Each of the Top One Percent Networkers that are featured in this book were interviewed by Pat Petrini about not only their morning routines, but their tips, techniques and strategies that have been critical in helping them become the best of the best in network marketing.

For your free and exclusive interview with Jessica, go to www. TMMforNetworkMarketers.com/Jessica

— 4 —

NOT-SO-OBVIOUS NETWORK MARKETING PRINCIPLE #1:

SELF-LEADERSHIP

*"Argue for your limitations, and sure enough they're
yours."*
—RICHARD BACH, New York Times Best-
Selling Author

You're a network marketer, and I know you know how hard
(read: impossible) it is to sell others on something if you
aren't sold on it yourself.

Your job as a network marketer is to find people who can benefit from the products and/or services that you offer, including those
who might desire the opportunity to be a part of your team. If
you don't believe your business or products are top-shelf, it will be
impossible to convince others to join you or purchase from you.

You lead your prospective customers and business partners to
make the best buying decisions for them by guiding them through
all of their options. And just as it's impossible to sell something if
you don't believe in it yourself, or to convince someone to build a
business by your side if you don't love it with all of your heart and

soul, it's impossible to lead others if you don't know how to effectively lead yourself.

To find the happiness and success you desire and deserve, you must master the key principles of self-leadership. To grow your network marketing business, in other words, you need to grow yourself.

Andrew Bryant, founder of Self-Leadership International, summed it up this way: "Self-leadership is the practice of intentionally influencing your thinking, feelings, and behaviors to achieve your objective(s). It is having a developed sense of who you are, what you can do, and where you are going combined with the ability to influence your communication, emotions, and behaviors on the way to getting there."

Before I reveal the key principles of self-leadership, I want to share with you what I've discovered about the crucial role that mindset plays as the foundation of effective self-leadership. Your past beliefs, self-image, and the ability to collaborate with and rely upon others at integral times will factor into your ability to excel as a self-leader.

Be Aware and Skeptical of Your Self-Imposed Limitations

You may be holding onto false limiting beliefs that are subconsciously interfering with your ability to achieve your business goals.

For example, you may be someone who repeats, "I wish I was more motivated" or "I wish I were better at getting appointments," yet in reality you are more than capable of generating motivation and filling your calendar with appointments. Thinking of yourself as less than capable is assuming imminent failure and simultaneously thwarting your ability to succeed.

Effective self-leaders closely examine their beliefs, decide which ones serve them, and eliminate the ones that don't.

When you find yourself stating anything that sounds like a limiting belief, from "I don't have enough time," to "I could never do that," pause and turn your self-limiting statements into empower-

ns, such as: *Where can I find more time in my schedule?*
I do that?

, this allows you to tap into your inborn creativity and
y to make anything happen. There's always a way, when
you're committed.

See Yourself as Better than You've Ever Been

As Hal wrote in *The Miracle Morning*, most of us suffer from
Rearview Mirror Syndrome, limiting our current and future results
based on who we were in the past. You must remember, although
*where you are is a result of who you were, where you go depends entirely
on who you choose to be from this moment forward.*

All successful network marketers—especially the top 1 percent—at one point made the choice to see themselves as better
than they had ever been before. They stopped maintaining limiting
beliefs based on their past, and instead started forming their beliefs
based on their unlimited potential.

One of the best ways to do this is to follow the four-step formula for creating affirmations that was outlined in chapter 3. Be
sure to create affirmations that reinforce what's possible for you and
remind you of whom you're committed to becoming.

Actively Seek Support

I've coached hundreds of people through the processes of iden-
tifying their areas of strength and weaknesses, coming to grips with
their innate talents and abilities, and engaging the support they
need. I've found that those who struggle the most are those who
suffer in silence: they assume everyone else has greater capabilities,
and they all but refuse to seek help and assistance.

If that describes you, then this might help: every single person
who was interviewed for this book is not only a true top 1 percent
achiever, but each has a team that supports them. They know what
they excel at, and they know where they fall short. Not only have
they eventually embraced the gaps and found solutions, they are
just fine with their humanity.

Self-leaders know they need a team to provide the support to get things done. You might need administrative support, for example, so you can do what you do best: grow your business! You may need accountability support to overcome your tendency to procrastinate. We all need support in different areas of our lives, and great self-leaders understand that and use it to their benefit.

The Five Core Principles of Self-Leadership

To grow, and become a top achiever, you'll need to become a top self-leader. My favorite way to cut the learning curve in half and decrease the time it takes for you to reach the top 1 percent is to model the traits and behaviors of those who have reached the top before you.

During my eleven years in network marketing, I've seen many leaders and a myriad of effective strategies. Here are the five I believe will shave years off of your pursuit of self-leadership excellence:

1. Take 100 Percent Responsibility
2. Become Financially Free
3. Put Fitness First
4. Systematize Your World
5. Commit to Your Process

Principle #1: Take 100 Percent Responsibility

Here's the hard truth: If you're not living the life and achieving the goals you want right now, it's all on you.

The sooner you take ownership of that fact, the sooner you'll begin to move forward. This isn't meant to be harsh. The most successful people in the world are rarely victims. In fact, one of the reasons they are successful is that they take absolute, total, and complete responsibility for each and every single thing in their lives, whether it's personal or professional, good or bad, their job or someone else's.

While average people waste their time blaming and complaining, achievers are busy creating the results and circumstances they want for their lives. While mediocre network marketers complain to their team that none of their prospects are buying for *this* reason or *that* reason and no one is interested in joining their business, successful network marketers have taken responsibility for finding the right prospects and, more importantly, acquiring the skills necessary to build volume and get people started correctly. They're so busy working that they don't have time to complain. I've heard Hal say the following during one of his keynote speeches: "The moment you take 100 percent responsibility for *everything* in your life is the same moment you claim the power to change *anything* in your life. But you must understand that responsibility is not the same thing as blame. Blame determines who is at fault for something; responsibility determines who is committed to improving a situation. It rarely matters who is at fault; what matters is that YOU are committed to improving your situation." He's right. And it's so empowering when you truly start to act accordingly. Suddenly, life is in your control.

When you take true ownership of your life, there's no time for discussing whose fault something is, or who gets the blame. Playing the blame game is easy, but there's no longer any place for it in your life. Finding reasons for why you didn't meet your group volume goals is for the other guy, not you! You own your results; you make them happen. You always have a choice about how you respond or react in any and every situation.

Here's the psychological shift I suggest you make: take ownership and stewardship over all of your decisions, actions, and outcomes, starting right now. Replace unnecessary blame with total responsibility. From now on, there's no doubt about who is at the wheel, and who is responsible for all of your results. You make the calls, do the follow up, decide the outcomes you want, and you get them. Your results are 100 percent your responsibility. Right? The reality is that you can't change what's in the past, but the good news is that you can change everything else.

Remember: you are in the position of power, you are ⅰ trol, and there are no limits to what you can accomplish.

Principle #2: Aim To Become Financially Free and Act Accordingly

How is your financial situation? Are you earning significantly more money each month than you need to survive? Are you able to save, invest, and share part of your income on a regular basis? Are you debt-free with a large reserve that allows you to capitalize on opportunities that come your way and ride out unexpected challenges? If so, congratulations: you're among a very small percentage of people who live their lives from a place of abundance.

If not, don't be too hard on yourself; you're not alone. The majority of people have less than $10,000 to their name, and an average of $16,000 in unsecured debt. No judgment here if this describes you; I'm simply going to point you right back to Principle #1 and encourage you to take 100 percent responsibility for your financial situation. I've seen and heard every reason for someone to dive deep into debt, fail to save, and not have a nest egg. None of those matter now. Yes, the best time to have started saving a percentage of your income was five, ten, or even twenty years ago. But the next best time is right now. Whether you're 20, or 40, or 60 years old, it's never too late to take control of your personal finances. You'll find an incredible boost in energy from taking charge, and you'll be able to use your accumulated savings to create even more wealth because you'll actually have money to invest in new opportunities. Sounds good, right?

There's a good chance that the decision to become a network marketer was partially driven by a desire for financial freedom, but it is going to take more than that. I've seen *many* network marketers make millions of dollars and then wind up dead broke because of poor financial decisions. It turns out that learning how to make money is only half the battle. Learning how to *keep* it by saving and investing wisely is the second part of the puzzle.

...m isn't something you achieve overnight. It is a ...the mindset and the habits *now* that will take ...hat leads to financial freedom.

steps you can do right now to get you started

1. Set aside 10 percent of your income to save and invest. In fact, I recommend that you start by taking 10 percent of whatever you have in the bank right now and putting it in a savings account. (Go ahead, I'll wait.) Make whatever adjustments you need to make to your lifestyle to be able to live off of 90 percent of your current income.

2. Take another 10 percent and give it away. Most wealthy people give a percentage of their income to causes they believe in. But you don't have to wait until you're wealthy to start this practice. Tony Robbins said, "If you won't give $1 out of $10, you'll never give $1 million out of $10 million." Can't do 10 percent or the rent check will bounce? Fine, start with 5, 2, or 1 percent. It's not the amount that matters, but developing the mindset and creating the habit that will change your financial future and serve you for the rest of your life. You've got to start teaching your subconscious brain that can produce an abundant income, that there's more than enough, and that there is always more on the way.

3. Continuously educate yourself on the topic of money. It's one of the most important topics for you to master, and you can start by adding the following books, which cover various aspects of financial freedom, to your reading list:

- *Secrets of the Millionaire Mind: Mastering the Inner Game of Wealth* by T. Harv Eker
- *MONEY: Master the Game: 7 Simple Steps to Financial Freedom* by Tony Robbins
- *The Total Money Makeover: A Proven Plan for Financial Fitness* by Dave Ramsey
- *The Millionaire Fastlane: Crack the Code to Wealth and Live Rich for a Lifetime* by MJ DeMarco

- *Rich Dad Poor Dad* by Robert Kiyosaki

Principle #3: Put Fitness First

How's your health these days? Can you wake up before your alarm and do what's important, handle all the demands of the day, and put out the inevitable fires, all without ending the day exhausted and out of breath?

I discussed exercise as part of the Life S.A.V.E.R.S., and yes, I'm going to discuss it again right now. It's a fact that the state of your health and fitness is a huge factor in your energy and success levels—especially for network marketers. Doing what's required to sponsor a steady stream of new customers and recruit new team members requires a ton of energy. Network marketing truly is an energy sport. Like any sport, you need an almost endless supply of energy and stamina.

To conduct several presentations, constantly prospect for new customers, ensure that each and every client is satisfied, and inspire new business builders to get results can be exhausting. If you are overweight, out of shape, and constantly out of breath, setting bigger and bigger sales goals is, in my opinion, a recipe for disaster. You will not only feel like there's more month than money, but also like there's more day than energy.

The great news is that this is completely within your control!

Here are three practices of top performers that you can use to ensure that your health, fitness, and energy levels fully support your network marketing goals and objectives:

1. Eat and drink to win. Put very simply, everything you ingest either contributes to your health or detracts from it. Drinking water puts a check in the plus column; double shots of tequila won't. Eating fresh fruits and vegetables equals more plusses. Rolling through the drive-through to wolf down some fast food? Not so much. I know you know the drill. This isn't rocket science, but you do need to stop fooling yourself. Today, I encourage you to become aware of what you're eating and how it's affecting your per-

formance in the field. I'll dive deeper into this in the next chapter: Energy Engineering.

2. Sleep to win. Getting enough rest is as critical to performance as what you do or don't have in your diet. A good night's sleep provides the basis for a day of peak performance, clear thought, and successful presentation after successful presentation. You probably already know how many hours you need to be at your best. Reverse engineer your schedule so you are asleep in plenty of time to get all of the rest you need to perform at your best.

3. Exercise to win. It is no coincidence that you rarely see top performers who are terribly out of shape. Most invest 30-60 minutes of their time each day to hit the gym or the running trail because they understand the important role that daily exercise plays in their success. And while the "E" in S.A.V.E.R.S. ensures that you're going to start each day with 5-10 minutes of exercise, we recommended that you engage in 30-60 minute workouts at least three to five times per week. Doing so will ensure that your fitness level supports the energy and confidence you need to succeed.

Principle #4: Systematize Your World

I'm going to discuss in chapters 7–10 the strategies and systems I believe will be the most helpful to you as a network marketer. But you should know that effective self-leaders have systems for just about everything from work activities, such as scheduling, follow up, entering orders, and sending thank you cards, to personal activities, such as sleeping, eating, dealing with money, cars, and family responsibilities. Those systems make life easier and ensure they are always ready to perform.

Here are three examples of basic:

1. **Shutting Out The World**—In addition to my network marketing business, I have a real estate business (flipping houses), a real estate education business (teaching people to flip houses), and I'm an author now with my second book coming soon. As you can imagine, my time is very important to me just as I'm sure yours is to you. To avoid distraction and ensure that my attention is focused on the task at hand, my phone is almost always set on

Do Not Disturb mode. This blocks all incoming calls, texts, or notifications like email and social media. This is a simple thing that dramatically increases my daily productivity. Return calls and emails on your schedule, not everybody else's.

2. **Travel**—Hal, in addition to being a bestselling author, is a speaker who is on the road week after week, sharing *The Miracle Morning* message with audiences around the country and abroad. Collecting the items he needed for every trip was time-consuming, inefficient, and ineffective as he would often forget something at home or in his office. After the third time he forgot the charger for his computer and had to find an Apple store to buy a $99 replacement (ouch) or ask the front desk for a phone charger, shaver, or an extra set of cufflinks left behind by a previous guest, he'd had enough. He assembled a travel bag containing every single item he needs for his trips, and now he can leave at a moment's notice because his bag contains everything he needs to conduct business on the road: business cards, brochures, copies of his books, adaptors and chargers for his phone and computer, and even earplugs in case his hotel room neighbor is a noisy guest.

You'll know you need a system when you have a recurring challenge or you find that you're missing opportunities because you're unprepared. If you're walking out the door with just enough time to make an appointment only to discover you're running on fumes, you need a system for getting out the door earlier: pack your briefcase the night before, have your clothes already cleaned and pressed, set up the coffee maker, get up earlier, etc. Said another way, wherever you feel like you need to get your act together, you need a system. A life without systems is a life with unnecessary stress!

3. **Time-Blocking**—I am going to share something with you that will totally change your ability to produce consistent and spectacular network marketing results. Many of you may even want to slap yourselves when you hear this because it is something that almost all network marketers have been taught and almost none of them do effectively on a consistent basis: *You must have a pre-determined action plan filled with the activities that will get you to your*

goal, put all the activities into a time-blocked daily schedule, and live by it. If you write it in your schedule, you must do it. Doing this will help you own your results at a high level.

That's not to say you cannot have flexibility in your schedule. In fact, I strongly suggest that you plan plenty of family and recreation time in your calendar. You can move things on occasion as needed, but you must do all of the activities in your calendar. When you use time blocking, achieving your goals is no longer a matter of *if*, but only a matter of *when*.

One of the main reasons that this technique is so effective is because it takes the emotional roller coaster caused by results out of the decision making for your daily activities. How many times has an appointment gone bad and then ruined your day? Chances are, you accomplished nothing else that day. If you had followed your calendar though, and the calendar said networking event, writing ads, or making calls, and you were committed to the calendar, then you would have had a fruitful afternoon. Take control. Stop letting outside influences manage your calendar. Start blocking your time, and follow through, no matter what.

If you find you need additional support around this, send a copy of your calendar to a coach, your upline or an accountability partner and have them hold you accountable. Your commitment to this one skill will allow you to take full responsibility for your level of activity and create results.

There's no need to reinvent the wheel to create a system—someone has struggled with and overcome any challenge you are faced with. If ideas escape you, find the closest person who excels at what you struggle with and ask their advice! They may be on the same path as you, just a little further ahead. Soon, you'll have the systems you need and the extra energy they provide.

Principle #5: Commit to Your Process

If there is any not-so-obvious secret to success, this is it: Commit to your process (without being emotionally attached to your results). Every result that you desire—from improving your physique to increasing the size of your business—is preceded by a process that is required to produce the result. When you define YOUR process, and commit to it for an extended period of time, the results take care of themselves. There's no need to stress or worry about how a day, week, or even a month goes—so long as you're committed to your process for the long haul.

Yet, as human beings, it is natural for us to be emotionally attached to our short-term results. As network marketers, we can let a bad day on the phone or a "no, I'm not going to join your business" cause us to feel bad. We allow a discouraging day of appointments to discourage us. When our numbers are down, we feel down. We ride the emotional roller coaster of being a network marketer, and our emotional attachment to our results negatively affects our commitment to our process. But does it have to be that way? It absolutely does not.

Hal had this realization at just 21 years old, to which he credits much of his selling success. "I realized that if I committed to making X number of calls each day (my process), the law of averages (which we will discuss more in chapter 10) would all but ensure that I could count on Y number of sales each month, quarter, and year. So, it only made sense to commit to my process—a predetermined number of daily calls—and there was no reason to worry or to get so stressed out over my day-to-day results. Then I realized that if I simply increased my number of daily calls by any percentage, I would, by default, increase my sales (and my income) by the same percentage. Double my calls, and I would double my sales. It almost seemed too simple, but it worked like clockwork."

Network marketers who produce consistent results, that top 1 percent who are the very best at putting impressive sales and recruiting numbers on the board, simply take consistent action. To become a top one-percenter, you can't take *some* action. You can't take a *little* action. You can't do it only when you feel like it or only when you're inspired. You have to define your daily process and take consistent action, day in and day out, for an extended period of time. The good news is that someday you will be on such a roll and have so much momentum that you may not need to work as hard. As your skill and your numbers improve, your process can be tweaked and upgraded to achieve greater results.

But until that day comes, until you have a major capital reserve, have eliminated all debt, and gotten yourself to where you really want to be, you've got to put in the time and effort. There are no exceptions and no substitutions for committing to your process (without being emotionally attached to your results).

In the chapters that follow, I'll give you the insight and direction you need to take consistent action. For now, you'll need to prepare your mind to keep going—even when the results you want aren't coming fast enough—and to have the stamina to withstand plenty of rejection and disappointment. The top 1 percent aren't the very best because they make a few calls or talk to a few people about the business opportunity on a semi-regular basis. They are consistent, persistent, and unfailing in their dedication to taking action every single day, and you need to be the same!

Where is Your Self-Discipline?

Self-discipline is the ability to make yourself do the things that you know are in your long-term best interest. In many cases, it is simply the ability to resist short-term temptation. When used wisely and with common sense, self-discipline becomes one of the most important tools for self-improvement and network marketing success.

Self-discipline is helpful when addressing addictions or any kind of incongruous behavior. It will improve your relationships, help you develop patience and tolerance, and is important for attaining success and happiness. Imagine having the self-discipline to handle anything that comes your way.

How does self-discipline help you? Let me count the ways...

- Keeps in check self-destructive, addictive, obsessive, and compulsive behavior.
- Gives you a sense of mastery and balance in your life.

- Helps to keep inappropriate emotional responses in check.
- Eliminates feelings of helplessness and dependency on others.
- Helps to manifest mental and emotional detachment (really important in network marketing!), which contributes to peace of mind.
- Enables you to control your moods and reject negative feelings and thoughts.
- Strengthens self-esteem, confidence, inner strength, self-mastery, and willpower.
- Enables you to take charge of your life.
- Makes you an emotionally stable human being.

How to Develop Self-Control

1. First, you need to identify the areas of your life where you need to gain more self-discipline. Where do you find yourself lacking in self-discipline?

Possible areas could be:

- Eating
- Spending
- Drinking
- Working
- Gambling
- Smoking
- Obsessive behavior
- Procrastinating
- Loving (yes, love requires discipline in the long term)

2. Try to identify the emotions that indicate a lack of control, such as anger, dissatisfaction, unhappiness, resentment, pleasure, or fear.

3. Identify the thoughts and beliefs that push you to behave in an uncontrolled manner.

4.   Several times a day, especially when you need to exert self-discipline, repeat one of the following affirmations (or create one of your own for the situation) for one or two minutes:

- I am fully in control of myself.
- I have the power to choose my emotions, thoughts, and actions.
- Self-discipline brings me inner strength and leads me to success.
- I am in charge of my behavior.
- I am the master of my life.
- Self-discipline is fun and pleasurable.

5.   Use the "V" in your Life S.A.V.E.R.S. to visualize yourself acting with self-discipline. Think of an instance where you usually act with a lack of discipline and visualize yourself acting calmly and with self-mastery.

Your Self-Leadership Acceleration Steps

Remember, taking your business to the next level starts with taking yourself to the next level. Developing self-leadership puts you in control of your life. It eliminates the victim mentality and ensures you make measurable and swift progress toward network marketing success.

Step One: Review and integrate the Five Core Principles of Self-Leadership:

1. **Take 100 Percent Responsibility.** Remember, the moment you accept responsibility for *everything* in your life is the moment you claim the power to change *anything* in your life. Your success is 100 percent up to you.

2. **Become Financially Free.** Begin to develop the mindset and habits that will inevitably lead you to a life of financial freedom, including saving a minimum of 10 percent of your income and continuing to educate yourself on the topic of money.

3. **Put Fitness First.** If daily fitness isn't already a priority in your life, make it so. In addition to your morning exercise, block time for longer, 30-60 minute workouts three to five times each week.

4. **Systematize Your World.** Start putting systems and time-blocked schedules in place so that every day your result-producing processes have been predetermined and your success is virtually guaranteed. It's then simply a matter of waking up and following through with what you've planned to do when you planned to do it.

5. **Commit to Your Process.** Remember Hal's not-so-obvious secret to success: *Commit to your process without being emotionally attached to your results.* Determine which activities you are 100 percent in control of (e.g., prospecting calls) that ultimately produce your results. This is YOUR process. Make your success inevitable by staying committed to your process each day, and let go of any emotional attachment to your short term results since it's your commitment to your (and your team's) daily process that will determine your volume total at the end of the month, quarter, and year.

Step Two: Develop your self-control and upgrade your self-image by using affirmations and visualization. Be sure to customize both at your earliest opportunity—it takes time to see results and the sooner you start, the sooner you'll notice improvements.

TOP ONE PERCENT NETWORKER INTERVIEW

Vincent Ortega Jr.

www.VincentOrtegaJr.Com

Facebook.com/VincentOrtegaJr

Periscope: @vincentortegajr

Instagram.com/VincentOrtegaJr

Twitter.com/VincentOrtegaJr

Linkedin.com/in/VincentOrtegaJr

Snapchat: @vincentortegajr

Before network marketing, Vince was a college athlete (supposed to become pro) because he had a 95mph fastball and professional curveball/slider.

He got started in network marketing around the age of 24 because his Mom (a National Director in Mary Kay) said one of her friend's sons was doing awesome in a health company.

He saw his mom become a massive success story and amazing entrepreneur, so he said, "why not?" and gave it a shot.

Today, Vincent Ortega Jr has created a 7-figure online business & now coaches over 150,000 entrepreneurs from all over the world on how to model his proven online systems to sell their products faster & easier.

Vincent's Miracle Morning & Daily Rituals:

• Wake up at 7am & have a protein shake and vitamins

• Listen to inspiration, motivation & wisdom for 30 minutes

• Workout at 8am - mainly swimming

• Come back, eat and answer team emails and questions from 9:30am-10am

• Start writing email/thought for the day from 10am-11am - I get inspired to write by answering questions and problems from my team over the last 30 minutes to an hour. I get inspired to usually talk about overcoming the obstacles that are holding some of my team members back. I also share the massive results that happened the day prior from my team mates.

- I might also record a video, upload it to YouTube or Facebook and drive my email list and network to that video.

- 11am - Hangout with my family for at least an hour and then decide to come back to work if I choose so for the rest of the day.

BONUS INTERVIEW FOR *MIRACLE MORNING FOR NETWORK MARKETING* READERS

Each of the Top One Percent Networkers that are featured in this book were interviewed by Pat Petrini about not only their morning routines, but their tips, techniques and strategies that have been critical in helping them become the best of the best in network marketing.

For your free and exclusive interview with Vincent, go to www.TMMforNetworkMarketers.com/vincent

TOP ONE PERCENT NETWORKER INTERVIEW

Ann Sieg

www.TheRenegadeBlog.com

Facebook.com/annsiegpage

YouTube.com/user/annsieg

Linkedin.com/in/annsieg

Pinterest.com/annsieg

Ann runs a family run business with her eldest son and husband. They've been working together as a team for the last ten years building their business online.

With her very first online MLM company, she became the top producer and was responsible for 80% of the company's sales volume.

A few of Ann's accomplishments:

- She went from $2,000 a month to over $90,000 in sales in under three months with her first online MLM.

- She has become the top producer of nearly every MLM she's built over the last ten years.

- She's authored three widely read books and is considered the godmother of attraction marketing. Her three popular books are The 7 Seven Great Lies of Network Marketing, The Renegade Network Marketer and The Attraction Marketer's Manifesto.

- She developed a subscriber list of 400,000 people worldwide and through her training and resources she's developed many 6, 7 and 8 figure income earners.

Ann's Miracle Morning & Daily Rituals:

• My morning begins the night before by writing down my list of "to dos" ranked in importance by what are the highest income producing activities. I have done this for many years. It was my mom who modeled this for me. I have a training on this for my community. We call it EOD - End of Day report. This has been a huge game changer for many of my members because previously they never tracked their activity to properly see cause and effect.

• Giving gratitude and thanks every night while in bed is mainstay along with giving thanks and gratitude first thing in the morning. It's a great time to be alive! There is nothing more toxic than a negative attitude. I have my parents and upbringing to thank for helping me in this way. I also have learned the importance of humility through my work at a nursing home while I was a young adult. I am truly grateful for everything that I have and most importantly my health. We can lose any of these at any moment.

• I do a fair amount of pep talk to myself. In the morning it's, "Let's get to work!" but not before my other routines. I am my biggest cheerleader. I have taught my students to learn to self regulate and self coach yourself to success. You can't always have someone there guiding and coaching you along the way. I developed my education philosophy from my parents who were both teachers. I strongly believe in self education. As a coach and mentor I help people to think and problem solve for themselves.

• After waking up and giving thanks (while still in bed) I check for email and skype messages from my staff. I am the CEO and always seek to be on top of the needs of my team. My staff is a top priority for me. In this way I never fall behind in communication with my team. I have my team to thank for my success. The team can only be as great as its leader. I am acutely aware of this with me as their primary role model. I must lead for them to follow.

• First thing in the morning I have a glass of room temperature water with 2 teaspoons of vinegar. I drink this while going through my morning routine of reading a powerful mindset book and then my devotional reading. I set my iphone timer for 10 minutes of each. Vinegar water helps with setting the body at the proper PH level.

- I am not a morning workout person. I am a late afternoon workout person. Though I do occasionally walk with my husband in the early morning. He walks every morning for 20-30 minutes.

- We have switched to an entirely anti-inflammatory diet so the foods we eat are considerably different than the average American. We do not eat any white sugar, white flour or white rice. We eat a lot of greens and vegetables.

- I have a greens drink every day along with a protein drink. We prepare nearly all of our food. We eat little to no processed food.

- Since transitioning into an anti-inflammatory diet I have since eliminated wine and coffee from my diet.

- I have a gym membership and personal trainer. I was a sports coach for 15 years and have a huge appreciation for physical fitness. I take the same approach to athletics into the business world. I often talk about becoming a business athlete and make parallels from the sports world. In many regards the disciplines are the same. One of my favorite books on this topic is "The Power of Engagement" by Jim Loehr and Tony Schwartz.

- Finally to say I have an amazing husband who has supported me in all my endeavors. For me it is critical to show ongoing appreciation, love and support to those who help me in my journey. My husband is that person. Second to that is my head coach who brought me online over 11 years ago. My recommendation is if you don't have a support network is you really need to make that a top priority. You simply cannot become a successful person without it. This is why I have developed out a huge leadership team of over 45 leaders who help give into the community I've developed. I do not believe in the "go it alone" mindset. It's a failed model for an old age. The new model is being in communities of like-minded people. The internet has made that possible more than ever before.

- As I say, "It's a great time to be alive!"

BONUS INTERVIEW FOR *MIRACLE MORNING FOR NETWORK MARKETING* READERS

Each of the Top One Percent Networkers that are featured in this book were interviewed by Pat Petrini about not only their morning routines, but their tips, techniques and strategies that have been critical in helping them become the best of the best in network marketing.

For your free and exclusive interview with Ann, go to www.TMMforNetworkMarketers.com/Ann

— 5 —

Not-So-Obvious Network Marketing Principle #2:

ENERGY ENGINEERING

"How do you become more productive? Work out."
–SIR RICHARD BRANSON, Billionaire and
Founder of The Virgin Group

As a network marketer, you live and die by your own steam. You eat what you kill, as they say. Most of the time, if you don't sell your products and grow your team, *you don't get paid.*

The trouble, though, isn't that it's all up to you. It's that on some days—and I know you've had those days—you wake up and you just don't have the energy or the motivation to hunt. To get out there on those days and face uncertainty, rejection, and disappointment is no easy task. The good days take energy, enthusiasm, and persistence. The hard days? They take all that and more.

Network marketing requires an abundance of energy. There's no way around it. You can have the best product, the most amazing prospects, the hottest leads, and the most amazing marketing support—but if you don't have the *energy* to take advantage of them, you might as well have no product or opportunity at all. If you want to maximize your network marketing, you need energy—the more the better, and the more *consistent* the better. After all

- Energy helps you get out there day after day.

- Energy is contagious—it spreads from you to your clients and prospects like a positive virus, creating symptoms of enthusiasm and yes responses everywhere.

- Energy is a vaccine against rejection and disappointment. Get enough of it, and you're almost permanently inoculated against negativity.

The question then becomes, *how do you generate and maintain a high level of sustainable energy on demand?*

When I'm struggling with energy issues, I can compensate with caffeine and other stimulants, and they'll work for a while … until I crash. You may have noticed the same thing. You can lean on stimulants to build up energy for a short while, but then the energy seems to fall off just when you need it the most.

If you have been, until now, fueling yourself on coffee and pure determination, you haven't even begun to reach the heights of achievement that are possible when you build and tap into the energy you have within you.

Natural Energy Cycles

The first thing to understand about energy is that that the goal isn't to be running at full speed all the time. It isn't practical to maintain a constant, full-out energy level. As human beings, there is a natural ebb and flow to our energy levels. Network marketing, it turns out, is the same. It also goes through intense cycles, such as during the holidays, push periods, major deadlines, and even quota busters. The trick with energy is to marry, or at least try to sync up, your energy cycles with your work cycles. You will need to access deeper wells of energy during these particularly intense times throughout your year, and allow yourself the time to rest, rejuvenate, and recharge when the intensity lessens.

Just like houseplants need water, our energy reserves need regular replenishing. You can go full tilt for long periods of time, but eventually your mind, body, and spirit will need to be refilled. Instead of getting to the point of overwhelm, burn out, and maximum stress, why not become proactive about your energy levels and have an auto-recharge system in place?

If you have resigned yourself to the fact that you will most likely be tired, cranky, behind on your to do list, out of shape, and unhappy, I have some great news.

Being continually exhausted is not only unacceptable, *you don't have to settle for it*. There are a few simple ways to get what you need and want—enough rest, time to replenish and recharge, and inner peace and happiness. A tall order? Yes. Impossible? Heck, no!

This is about strategically engineering your life for optimum and sustainable physical, mental, and emotional energy. Here are the three principles I follow to keep my energy reserves at maximum capacity and on tap for whenever I need them.

1. Sleep Smarter

Sleep more, achieve more. That might be the most counter-intuitive business mantra you'll ever hear, but it's true. The body needs enough shut-eye each night to function properly and to recharge after a demanding day. Sleep also plays a critical role in immune function, metabolism, memory, learning, and other vital bodily functions. It's when the body does the majority of its repairing, healing, resting, and growing.

If you don't sleep enough, you're gradually wearing yourself, and your ability to grow your business, down.

Sleeping Versus Sleeping *Enough*

But how much is enough? There is a big difference between the amount of sleep you can get by on and the amount you need to function optimally. Researchers at the University of California, San Francisco discovered that some people have a gene that enables them to do well on six hours of sleep a night. This gene, however, is very rare, appearing in less than 3 percent of the population. For the other 97 percent of us, six hours doesn't come close to cutting it. Just because you're able to function on five to six hours of sleep doesn't mean you wouldn't feel a lot better and actually get more done if you spent an extra hour or two in bed.

That may sound counterintuitive. I can almost hear you thinking, *Spend more time in bed and get more done? How does that work?* But it has been well documented that enough sleep allows the body to function at higher levels of performance. You'll not only work better and faster, but your attitude will improve, too.

The amount of rest each individual needs every night differs, but research shows that the average adult needs approximately seven to eight hours of sleep to restore the energy it takes to handle all of the demands of living each day.

I have been conditioned, as many of us have, to think I need eight to ten hours of sleep. In fact, sometimes I need less, and sometimes I need more. The best way to figure out if you're meeting your sleep needs is to evaluate how you feel as you go about your day. If you're logging enough hours, you'll feel energetic and alert all day long, from the moment you wake up until your regular bedtime. If you're not, you'll reach for caffeine or sugar mid-morning or mid-afternoon ... or both.

If you're like most people, when you don't get enough rest, you have difficulty concentrating, thinking clearly, and even remembering things. You might notice your ineffectiveness or inefficiencies at home or at work or even blame these missteps on your busy schedule. The more sleep you miss, the more pronounced your symptoms become.

In addition, a lack of rest and relaxation can really work a number on your mood. Network marketing is no place for crankiness! It is a scientific fact that when individuals miss out on good nightly rest, their personalities are affected, and they are generally grumpier, less patient, and snap at people more easily. The result of missing out on critical, much-needed rest might make you a bear to be around, which is not much fun for anyone, yourself included.

Most adults cut back on their sleep to pack more activities into their day. As you run against the clock to beat deadlines, you might be tempted to skimp on sleep in order to get more done. Unfortunately, lack of sleep can cause the body to run down, which allows illness, viruses, and diseases the tiny opening they need to attack the body. When you are sleep deprived, your immune system can become compromised, and is susceptible to just about anything. Eventually, lack of rest can cause illness that leads to missed days or even weeks of work. That's no way to attempt to grow your business.

On the flip side, when you get enough sleep, your body runs as it should, you're pleasant to be around, and your immune system is stronger. And that's precisely when you'll make more sales and attract more people into your business. Think of good sleep as the time when you turn on your inner magnet. Wake up rested and in a great mood because of your Life S.A.V.E.R.S., and you'll attract more business because a happy network marketer is also a rich one.

The True Benefits of Sleep

You may not realize how powerful sleep actually is. While you're happily wandering through your dreams, sleep is doing some hard work on your behalf and delivering a host of amazing benefits.

Improve your memory. Your mind is surprisingly busy while you snooze. During sleep you clean out damaging toxins that are by-products of brain function during the day, strengthen memories and practice skills learned while you were awake through a process called consolidation.

"If you are trying to learn something, whether it's physical or mental, you learn it to a certain point with practice," says Dr. David Rapoport, who is an associate professor at NYU Langone Medical Center and a sleep expert, "but something happens while you sleep that makes you learn it better."

In other words, if you're trying to learn something new, whether it's Spanish, a new tennis swing, or the specifications of a new product in your arsenal, you'll perform better when you get adequate sleep.

Live longer. Too much or too little sleep is associated with a shorter life span, although it's not clear if it's a cause or an effect. In a 2010 study of women ages 50-79, more deaths occurred in women who got fewer than five hours or more than six-and-a-half hours of sleep per night. Getting the right amount of sleep is a good idea for your long-term health.

Be more creative. Get a good night's sleep before getting out the easel and paintbrushes or the pen and paper. In addition to consolidating memories or making them stronger, your brain appears to reorganize and restructure them, which may result in more creativity as well.

Researchers at Harvard University and Boston College found that people seem to strengthen the emotional components of a memory during sleep, which may help spur the creative process.

Attain and maintain a healthy weight more easily. If you're overweight, you won't have the same energy levels as those at a healthy weight. If you are changing your lifestyle to include more exercise and diet changes, you'll want to plan an earlier bedtime. Putting additional physical demands on your body means you will need to counter-balance those demands with enough rest.

The good news: researchers at the University of Chicago found that dieters who were well-rested lost more fat—up to 56 percent more—than those who were sleep deprived, who lost more muscle mass. Dieters in the study also felt hungrier when they got less sleep. Sleep and metabolism are controlled by the same sectors of the brain, and when you are sleepy, certain hormones go up in your blood, and those same hormones drive appetite.

Feel less stressed. When it comes to our health, stress and sleep are closely connected, and both can affect cardiovascular health. Sleep can definitely reduce stress levels, and with that comes better control of blood pressure. It is also believed that sleep affects cholesterol levels, which play a significant role in heart disease.

Avoid mistakes and accidents. The National Highway Traffic Safety Administration reported in 2009 that being tired accounted for the highest number of fatal, single-car, run-off-the-road crashes due to the driver's performance—even more than alcohol! Sleepiness is grossly underrated as a problem by most people, but the cost to society is enormous. Lack of sleep affects reaction time and decision-making.

If insufficient sleep for only one night can be as detrimental to your driving ability as having an alcoholic drink, imagine how it affects your ability to maintain the focus necessary to become a top network marketer.

So, how many hours of sleep do you *really* need? You tell me, because only you truly know how much sleep you need in order to hit home run after home run. Now, if you really struggle with falling or staying asleep, and it is a concern for you, I highly recommend getting a copy of Shawn Stevenson's book, *Sleep Smarter: 21 Proven Tips to Sleep Your Way to a Better Body, Better Health, and Bigger Success.* It's one of the best written and most researched books that I've seen on the topic of sleep.

2. Rest Your Mind

The conscious counterpart to sleep is *rest*. While some people use the terms interchangeably, they're really quite different. You might get eight hours of sleep, but if you spend all of your waking hours on the go, then you won't have any time to think or recharge your batteries. When you work all day, run from activity to activity after hours, and then finish with a quick dinner and a late bedtime, you don't allow for a period of rest.

Likewise, spending weekends taking the kids to soccer, volleyball, or basketball, then heading out to see a football game, going to church, singing in the choir, attending several birthday parties, etc., can do more harm than good. While each of these activities is great, maintaining a fully-packed schedule doesn't allow for time to recharge.

We live in a culture that perpetuates the belief that when our days are busy and exciting, we are more valuable, more important, or more alive. In truth, we are all of those things when we can be at peace within our own skin. Despite our best intentions to live balanced lives, the modern world demands that we are almost always connected and productive, and these demands can drain us emotionally, spiritually, and physically.

What if, instead of being constantly on the go, you valued intentional quiet time, sacred space, and silence? How would that change your life, parenting abilities, and ability to achieve network marketing success?

It may seem counterintuitive to take time out when your to-do list is a mile long, but the fact is that more rest is a pre-requisite to truly productive work.

Research proves that rest melts your stress away. Practices like yoga and meditation also lower heart rates, blood pressure, and oxygen consumption and alleviate hypertension, arthritis, insomnia, depression, infertility, cancer, and anxiety. The spiritual benefits of resting are profound. Slowing down and getting quiet means you can actually hear your own wisdom, your inner knowledge, and your inner voice. Rest and its close sibling, relaxation, allow us to reconnect with the world in and around us, inviting ease in our lives and a sense of contentment.

And yes, in case you're wondering, you'll be more productive, nicer to your friends and family members (not to mention your prospects and clients), and in general much happier as well. When we rest, it's like letting the earth lie fallow rather than constantly planting and harvesting. Our personal batteries need to be recharged. The best way is to recharge them is to truly and simply rest.

Easy Ways to Rest

Most of us confuse rest with recreation. To rest, we do things like hike, garden, work out, or even party. Any of these activities can only be termed restful because they are breaks from work, but truthfully they are not, and cannot, be defined as rest.

Rest has been defined as a kind of waking sleep, experienced while you are alert and aware. Rest is the essential bridge to sleep, and we achieve rest and sleep the same way: by making space for them and allowing them to happen. Every living organism needs rest, including you. When we don't take the time to rest, eventually its absence takes a toll on the body.

- If you are using five minutes every morning during your Life S.A.V.E.R.S. to meditate or sit in silence, that is a great start.

- You can reserve Sundays or, if Sunday is a busy workday for you, choose another day of the week for rest. You can read, watch a movie, do something low-key with family, or even spend time alone. Try cooking at home, playing games with your kids, and enjoying each other's company.

- When you're driving, drive in silence: turn off the radio and stow your phone.

- Go for a walk without your ear buds in. Even a walk in nature without intention or goals, such as burning calories, can work.

- Turn off the television. Designate a half hour, an hour, or even half a day for silence. Try taking a few conscious breaths, during which you focus on the inhale and exhale or the space between breaths.

- You can also mindfully drink a cup of tea, read something inspirational, write in your journal, take a hot bath, or get a massage.

- Attend a retreat. It could be with your team, a group of friends, your church, any community with which you are involved, family, your spouse, or on your own in nature.

Even taking a nap is a powerful way to rest and recharge. If I'm feeling drained during the day for some reason and still have a long day ahead, I won't hesitate to hit the reset button with a 30–45 minute nap. Napping also can lead to better sleep patterns.

It's helpful to set a specific time for rest. Put boundaries around it so you can claim that time.

The Rest Habit

Rest certainly isn't something we're taught in school, and it may not come naturally at first. You may find you need to learn it and make it a habit. Practices, such as Yoga Nidra, restorative yoga, and voluntary silence, are powerful ways to go within and achieve restful states of being, particularly when you commit to practicing them regularly.

Learning different contemplative practices and bringing them into your everyday life is an effective way to deeply rest your body, mind, and spirit. Think of how much you and your network marketing career will benefit from your taking the time to care for yourself.

3. Eat for Energy

A low energy network marketer sells well below their potential, and when it comes to energy, food may play the most critical role of all. If you're like most people, you make your food choices based on taste first, and consequences second (if you consider them at all). Yet, what makes us happy when we eat doesn't always give us maximum energy.

There is nothing wrong with eating foods that taste good, but if you want to be truly healthy and have the energy to sell like a champion, **you must learn to value the energy consequences of the food you eat above the taste.** Digesting food is one of the most energy-draining processes the body endures (think about how exhausted you feel after a big meal, like Thanksgiving dinner). Thus, **eating living foods that contribute more energy to your body than they require to digest is the secret to maintaining extraordinary levels of energy** *all day long.*

Foods like bread, cooked meats, dairy products, and processed foods require a lot of energy to digest and contribute very little energy to your body, leaving you in an energy deficit. Foods like raw fruits, vegetables, nuts, and seeds typically give you more energy than they take, empowering you with an energy surplus to perform at your best.

I have shifted my view of food from that of a reward, treat, or comfort to that of fuel. I want to eat delicious, healthy foods that boost my energy levels and allow me to keep going as long as I need to go.

Don't get me wrong. I still enjoy certain foods that are not the healthiest choices, but I strategically reserve them for times when I don't need to maintain optimum energy levels, such as in the evenings and on weekends.

The easiest way for me to start making some better decisions about my eating was to start paying attention to the way I felt after eating certain foods. I set a timer for 60 minutes after I finished each meal. One hour later, my timer went off, and I assessed my energy level. It didn't take long for me to recognize which foods gave me the biggest power boost and which ones didn't. I can clearly tell the difference in my energy level on the days when I eat sushi or a salad and the day I cave for a chicken sandwich or some of that pizza that smells so good. I find that incorporating as many of the right foods as I can often stops me from snacking on the unhealthy foods.

The idea is to eat what you need to refuel and recharge your body—to give your body exactly what it needs to generate a sustained energy level. What would it be like to give your body what it needs to work and play for as long as you like? What would it be like to give yourself exactly what you truly deserve? Give yourself the gift of great health, consciously chosen through what you eat and drink.

If you are eating throughout the day almost as an afterthought, maybe hitting a drive-through after you've hit the point of being famished, it is time to start building a new strategy.

Give some thought to the following:

- Can I start to consciously consider the consequences of what I eat (both health and energy consequences) and value that above the taste?

- Can I keep water with me at all times so that I can hydrate with intention and purpose and avoid becoming dehydrated?

- Can I plan my meals in advance, including snacks, so I can combat any patterns I have that don't serve me?

Yes, you can do all of these and much more. Think about how much better your life will be and how much more energy you will have for your business when you become conscious and intentional about your eating and drinking habits.

- You will spend more time consciously thinking about food (and truly enjoying the food you eat).

- You will spend less money on food.

- You will eat less.

- You will get healthier and feel much better.

- Total bonus—you will settle at your natural weight effortlessly.

- Best bonus ever—you'll make more sales, recruit more team members, and make more money because you'll look and feel great!

Combining exercise, meditation, rest, and healthy food choices is a positive leap in the right direction for you and your network marketing career

Don't forget hydration. As part of your Miracle Morning, you'll have had your first glass of water at the start of the day. I recommend including a full glass of water with each meal, which makes it easier to get in the recommended eight to ten glasses a dayI intentionally refuel every three to four hours during the day. My regular meals consist of some form of protein and vegetables. I snack frequently on fruits, protein bars, chocolate covered raisins, or yogurt. I try to plan my best meals for the days I need to be the most productive.

I believe that eating great most of the time, combined with exercise, gives me the latitude to eat what I want some of the time. I believe I can eat whatever I want, just not always as much as I'd like. I've learned to taste everything, but to eat just enough that I'm satisfied.

In the end, here is the simple thing to remember: food is fuel. It serves to get us from the beginning of the day all the way to the end, feeling great and having plenty of energy. Food can be used as the fuel you need, and you can use it to your advantage: to give you the endless energy you need to be the extraordinary network marketer you are meant to be.

Practice, Practice, Practice

Keep in mind that when you try to adopt these three practices—to sleep, rest, and eat better—you may at first find adopting them to be uncomfortable. It can be like when you're flying in a jetliner at 30,000 feet: as soon as you start your descent, it almost always gets a little bumpy.

Your mind and body experience can be similar, and you may encounter some emotional turbulence. Many find it so uncomfortable that they flee that turbulence by quickly becoming busy again. Resist the urge to run from the discomfort.

The more you integrate periods of rest and silence into your daily life, the bigger the payoff will be. During more tranquil periods, perhaps you won't need to rest as much, but periods of intensity (such as meeting a huge quota or a big deadline) may require more rest and silence than usual.

As a network marketer, you're in the trenches by default. You'll need to schedule rest, recharging, silence, and self-care in the same way you schedule the other appointments in your life. The energy you get back will reward you many times over.

Now that you can create endless energy, what do you do with it? Unharnessed energy can be as detrimental as no energy at all. And that's why the next principle is just as important.

Your Energy Engineering Acceleration Steps

Step One: Make sleep a priority by choosing a consistent daily bedtime and wake up time. Decide when you will wake up to do your Miracle Morning, and then back your way into a bedtime that ensures that you will get enough sleep. Maintain a specific bedtime for a few weeks to get your body on a natural clock. After a couple of weeks, feel free to play with the number of hours you leave for sleeping to optimize your energy levels. (Try nighttime sleep meditations if you struggle with falling asleep once you actually make it to bed.)

Step Two: Incorporate time into your daily calendar to rest and recharge. For example, Hal takes a two-hour lunch break every day, which gives him time to play basketball—something he loves to do and that reenergizes him. What can you plan in your day that will reenergize you? In addition to your Miracle Morning routine, schedule regular daily periods to rest and recharge.

Step Three: Plan longer periods of time for relaxation, such as a weekly date night, a monthly overnight getaway, or an annual vacation. Many of us have cycles in our network marketing calendar, and we should plan our life cycles around them. Schedule at least a few weeks of vacation throughout the year, possibly even once a quarter. Schedule it (and pay for it) ahead of time, so you will actually take it.

Step Four: Start eating for energy. Try incorporating one new healthy meal into your diet each day. If you already have one healthy meal, try adding a second or try some new healthy snacks. And remember to keep water with you at all times so that you stay hydrated.

Advanced Step: Find ways to combine multiple practices. Plan a hike with friends or family or build a date night around preparing a healthy meal together.

TOP ONE PERCENT NETWORKER INTERVIEW

Mark Hoverson

www.MinuteWithMark.com

Instagram.com/markhoverson

Facebook.com/hoverson1

Mark Hoverson is an 8-Figure Adventurepreneur, Info-Marketer, and Dad of 4 rambunctious kids.

A few of Mark's accomplishments:

#1- His marketing & lifestyle "how to" videos have been viewed over 1,000,000 hours online.

#2- He started his business at a public library, while being $40,000 in credit card debt. Just 5 short years later he built an 8-Figure empire online.

#3- He spends the Winters in Arizona, and the Summers in North Dakota (where he grew up).

#4- PLAY is an integral part of Mark's daily routine. He uses PLAY almost as a carrot on a stick to motivate him to be as productive as possible during the day. It's his key to staying fresh & creative & inspired. It's ritualized. It's purposeful. It's a discipline as important to him as brushing his teeth or taking a shower. It's kinda like adult recess meets field trips meets business.

#5- He had an opportunity to consult and work for one of Donald Trump's companies, the NFL and other retail giants but turned those opportunities down because it wouldn't of aligned with his definition of lifestyle design.

Mark's Miracle Morning & Daily Rituals:

- Most mornings I will slam some Yerba Mate, Green Tea, or Coffee.

- Then I go to my library & select a few books that fit my appetite at that moment (just like picking a restaurant to eat at).

- I set my timer for 3-min and blast through the book as fast as I can...seeking only a few sentences or picture or info graphic that is new knowledge for me. 3-min max...no matter how engaged I am in the book.

- I do that process with all the books I have chosen.

- It's like an espresso shot for my mind.

- After that, I usually go for a run outside, or to the gym...with my mind buzzing...while on my run or workout...I listen to a podcast at double speed.

- Following all that...I begin my creative work for the day. I believe these kinds of rituals are what have allowed me to stay in momentum & resilient over the years.

BONUS INTERVIEW FOR *MIRACLE MORNING FOR NETWORK MARKETING* READERS

Each of the Top One Percent Networkers that are featured in this book were interviewed by Pat Petrini about not only their morning routines, but their tips, techniques and strategies that have been critical in helping them become the best of the best in network marketing.

For your free and exclusive interview with Mark, go to www.TMMforNetworkMarketers.com/Mark

TOP ONE PERCENT NETWORKER INTERVIEW

Jordan Hubbard Monroe

https://livesuccess.alten.com/vbc/66

Facebook.com/jordanhubb

Instagram: @monroewifey

Jordan grew up in a network marketing household. She earned a Division 1 basketball scholarship to the University of Portland and graduated with honors with a BA in English and a minor in Philosophy.

At the age of 21, she attended her first network marketing convention and realized her love for the business and jumped in.

By 2009, she had become the youngest Diamond Associate in her company at the age of 27.

In 2015, she was selected to represent her company in Nicaragua as an ambassador for ServeFirst.org with other groups like Vitamin Angels and Feed The Children distributed vitamins and nutrients to mal-nourished children.

She is also the Vice President of Synergy Business Alliance as well as an active member in Adventure Forward, a group that leads people on retreats to discover healing, connection, and guidance through the power of inner work and nature.

Jordan's Miracle Morning & Daily Rituals:

- My Miracle Morning starts the night before. Preparation makes the difference. Before going to bed, I make time to go over my calendar for the next day and make lists of "to-do's." Writing things down adds intention and accountability. I also keep a journal on my night stand, in case I get ideas or dreams and want to take notes. Inspiration comes in its own time.

- I make sure that I get a full 8 hours of sleep. For me, it makes all the difference in having a positive, productive, and energetic day. As I fall asleep I focus on the expectation that AWESOME is going to happen.

- My Rise and Shine time fluctuates between 545am and 730am depending on the day of the week. Monday, Wednesday and Friday I have early morning team calls and will begin my morning routine after they are complete. I enjoy being flexible with my routine start time, but remain diligent with my process.

- My morning ritual begins here: I turn on Kundalini Music (Snatam Kaur Pandora station) and begin by brushing my teeth. Relaxing by focusing on my breathing allows my mind to clear and provide space for the activities of the day.

- I make my bed every morning. My mother always wanted us to do this when we were little and I would fight it every chance I got. Now I see how making your bed truly sets the tone for the rest of the day.

- I draw back the curtains, say good morning to the world and say a prayer of gratitude. I never want to take for granted the space I hold in the world, so I do my best to celebrate it every morning.

- Making my way to the kitchen I straighten up the house. I love having a clean space to start the day. Again, my mom would be proud. Shocked, but proud!

- I also start the day with a mix of 33 different green foods from land and sea. Having something this full of nutrients first thing in the morning helps my brain work. It also jump starts my metabolism and keep my system alkaline.

- I then light my candles, do my morning reading and daily journaling. I journal because writing things down makes things real. And helps focus my intentions.

- Once my spirit, body, environment, and intention are set, I'm ready to engage the rest of the world.

- HI WORLD. I go over emails, texts, Facebook and Instagram messages and posts to stay connected. Half the world is awake while I slept - I wonder what they did?

- I go over my list from the night before, adding items that have come up from morning emails. This is also the time that I set my goals for the day. How many people am I going to reach out to, follow up with etc. The names and numbers are on my list. Being specific and rooted in reality is key.

- 9am M,W,F workout some days I prefer the classes offered at my gym at 12 and 430. Having energy to put into the day means that I have to store energy in my body.

- 10:15-11:15 - I begin connecting with my team. Start appointments made previously and making the calls and emails on my list. My success is ALL about RELATIONSHIP and staying Connected.

- I'm sure once my husband and I have children this routine will drastically change, but for now this is what I call my Miracle Morning!

BONUS INTERVIEW FOR *MIRACLE MORNING FOR NETWORK MARKETING* READERS

Each of the Top One Percent Networkers that are featured in this book were interviewed by Pat Petrini about not only their morning routines, but their tips, techniques and strategies that have been critical in helping them become the best of the best in network marketing.

For your free and exclusive interview with Jordan, go to www. TMMforNetworkMarketers.com/Jordan

— 6 —

Not-So-Obvious Network Marketing Principle #3:

UNWAVERING FOCUS

"The successful warrior is the average man, with laser-like focus."

–BRUCE LEE, World-Renowned Martial Artist and Actor

We've all met that person. You know—*that* person. The one who runs marathons, coaches little league, volunteers at her son's school lunch program, cooks great meals, and maybe writes a memoir on the side. And on top of all that? She's an incredible network marketer, ranking at the top of the company, winning awards at every convention, and knocking it out of the park when it comes to growing her business.

I bet you know someone like that—someone who just seems amazingly productive. What you might not realize, though, is exactly how they do it. Maybe you always thought they were lucky. Or gifted. Or connected. Or had the right personality. Or were born with super powers!

While those things can help when it comes to network marketing, I know from experience that the real superpower behind every unbelievably productive network marketer is *focus*.

Focus is the ability to maintain clarity about your highest priorities, take all of the energy you've learned to generate for yourself, channel it into what matters most, and keep it there, regardless of what is going on around you or how you feel.

When you harness the power of focus, you don't become superhuman, but you can achieve seemingly superhuman results. And the reasons for this are surprisingly straightforward.

- **Focus makes you more effective.** Being effective doesn't mean to do the most things or to do things the fastest. It means to do the *right* things. You engage in the activities that create forward momentum in your organization and generate sales.

- **Focus makes you more efficient.** Being efficient means to do things with the fewest resources, such as time, energy, or money. Every time your mind wanders away from your work, you waste those things—particularly time. In network marketing, time is money so every moment that your focus wavers is another dollar (or thousands of dollars) lost.

- **Focus makes you productive.** When you focus on your highest priorities, do the right things, and do them in the right way, you get more done with less effort. Too often we confuse being busy—engaged in activities that don't produce results—like cleaning your car or reorganizing your leads for the twelfth time this month—with being productive. By taking the steps that we're about to cover, you'll learn how to develop the habit of unwavering focus and join the ranks of the most productive network marketers in the world.

If you combine those benefits, you will sell and earn a *lot* more. Perhaps the greatest value of focus, however, is that it moves the needle not just in terms of your group volume, but also in every important area of your life. Rather than scattering your energy across multiple areas and getting mediocre results across the board, focus releases your untapped selling potential *and* improves your life.

Now let's turn your Miracle Morning to the task. Here are the three steps you need to turn your morning time into laser-focused, super-productive time.

1. Find Your Best Environment(s) to Focus.

Let's start here: *You need an environment that supports your commitment to unwavering focus.* It might be your home office, or it could be a coffee shop. No matter how modest, though, you need a place where you go to focus on conducting business.

Part of the reason for this is simple logistics. If your work is scattered from the trunk of your car to the kitchen counter, you simply can't be effective. A bigger reason, however, is that having a place where you focus triggers the habit of focusing. Trying to work at your kitchen table or make prospecting calls while sitting on your living room couch leaves you susceptible to being pulled into non-productive activities, like grabbing a bite to eat or watching television. Sit at the same desk to do great work at the same time every day, and soon enough you'll find yourself slipping into the zone just by sitting down in that place.

If you're on the road a lot, like me, then your car, your suitcase, your hotel rooms, and possibly random coffee shops are part of your focus space too. Build habits for how you pack and work on the road, and you can trigger great focus the same way you do at the office. When you are prepared and always have with you exactly what you need, you can work anywhere. I could even come and work on your couch or in your guestroom if necessary (just waiting on that invitation).

2. Clear the Clutter

Stuff is a focus killer, and it's our next stop on the journey. There are two kinds of clutter, mental and physical, and we all have them both. There are the things we carry around in our minds that need to be done, such as *my sister's birthday is coming up. I have to get her a gift and card.* Or *I had a great time at dinner the other night, I need to send the host a thank you note.* Or *I have to answer the email from my new client before I leave the office today.*

And there are things we carry around in our physical lives. Stacks of paper. Old magazines. Sticky notes. Clothes we never wear. The pile of junk in the garage. The trinkets, knick-knacks, and tokens that accumulate as we go through life.

Clutter of either type creates the equivalent of a heavy fog, and to become focused, you need to be able to *see*. To clear your vision, you'll want to get those mental items out of your head and collected so you can relieve the mental stress of trying to remember them. And then, you'll want to get those physical items out of your way.

Here's a simple process to help you clear the fog and create the clarity you need to focus.

- **Create a master to-do list.** You probably have lots of things that haven't been written down yet—start with those. And all those tiny little sticky notes that clutter your desk, computer screen, day timer, countertops, on the refrigerator … Are there other places? Put those notes and action items on your master list. Put them all into one central location, whether that's a physical journal or a list on your phone, so that you can completely clear your mental storage. Feeling better? Keep going; we're just getting started.

- **Purge your workspace.** Schedule a half (or full) day to go through every stack of paper, file folder stuffed with documents, and tray full of unopened mail … You get the gist. Throw out or shred what you don't need. Scan or file the ones that matter. Note in your journal any items that need your attention, that you cannot delegate, and pick a time in your schedule to complete them.

- **Declutter your life.** Clean up and clear out every drawer, closet, cabinet, and trunk that doesn't give you a sense of calm and peace when you see it. This includes your car. This could take a few hours or a few days. Schedule a short time each day until everything is complete. Saying, "I just need a weekend to declutter," is a sure way to never start. Pick a single drawer, and start there.

Getting physically and mentally organized will allow you to focus at a level you would never believe possible. It leaves your energy nowhere to go except to what *matters*.

3. Build Unwavering Focus

Once you identify your focus place and begin the process of decluttering your life, you should experience a remarkable increase in focus simply from clearing the fog in your mind.

Now, it's time to take things to the next level. I use three questions to improve my focus every day. They are:

- What's working that I should *keep doing* (or do more of)?
- What do I need to *start doing* to accelerate results?
- What do I need to immediately *stop doing* that's holding me back from going to the next level?

If you can answer those three questions and take action on the answers, you'll discover a whole new level of productivity you probably didn't think was possible. Let's look at each question in detail.

What Do You Need to *Keep* Doing (or do more of)?

Let's face it: not all network marketing tactics and strategies are created equal. Some work better than others. Some work for a period of time and then become less effective. Some even make things worse.

Right now, you're probably doing a lot of the right activities, and you'll be nodding right along as you read the coming chapters on the best business growth techniques. If you already know the things you're doing that are working, jot those down. Perhaps you're constantly prospecting and finding potential customers, for example. Put that on the "what's working" list. Perhaps a networking group is delivering great leads—add that to the list, too.

Make sure you're choosing things that are actually contributing to increasing your business. Consider the 80/20 Rule (originally the Pareto principle), which shows that roughly 80 percent of our results come from 20 percent of our efforts. Which 20 percent of your activities impact 80 percent of your results? It's easy to keep the things that you *like* doing, but this is network marketing—you need to make sure that the activities you're doing are directly related to producing leads, finding new business builders, and putting money in your bank account.

At the end of this chapter, you'll have an opportunity to capture in your journal the activities that are working. (Among them, I hope, will be that you've started doing the Life S.A.V.E.R.S. to take your personal development to the next level.) Everything that's on that list is a "keep doing" until it's replaced by something even more effective.

For all of the keep doing activities on your list, make sure you're completely honest with yourself about *what you need to be doing more of* (aka *what you're currently not doing enough of*). Are you averaging 20 prospecting calls per day, but haven't been reaching your sales and recruiting goals? Remember, any percentage that you increase your prospecting process, over an extended period of time, will result in that same percentage of an increase in the growth of your business overall. Go from 20 to 30 calls a day (a 50 percent increase), and it's only a matter of time before you see your business increase by roughly 50 percent, and much more as your team starts to duplicate your level of activity.

Keep doing what's working, and depending on how much more you want to sell, simply do *more* of what's working.

What Do You Need to *Start* Doing?

Once you've captured what's working—and determined what's working that you need to do more of—it's time to decide what *else* you can do that will accelerate your success.

I have a few top-shelf suggestions to prime the pump and get you started.

- Organize your database for targeted follow up and lead generation with past clients, current prospects, and your sphere of influence, so that you can consistently generate a stream of repeat sales and ongoing referrals. For comprehensive training on this topic, I highly recommend Michael J. Maher's bestselling book, *The 7 Levels of Communication*.

- Make sure your online presence is driving business. You can either use a service like *Likeable Hub* (https://likeablehub.com) or hire someone to optimize your social media accounts and to improve SEO, conversion rates, and content development.

- Create your *Foundational Schedule*—a recurring, ideal weekly schedule with a time-blocked calendar—so that every day when you wake up your highest priorities are already predetermined and planned. Then, make any necessary adjustments on Sunday night for the following week.

- Have whatever sales tools and materials you might need on hand at all times. Be sure to stock and re-stock so you are always prepared to help someone place their first order or get started in their new business venture.

- Once you've identified which activities you're spending time on that do *not* directly impact your growth, plan your first hire (or your next hire). This could be a personal assistant, a virtual assistant, an intern, or even someone new to the business who is eager to spend time with you and can help to save some cash. Realize that hiring someone to free up your time is an *investment*, not an expense. What would it be worth for you to free up enough of your time to increase your sales by 20–50 percent? It's time for you to start thinking bigger.

I caution you to not become overwhelmed here. Keep in mind that Rome wasn't built in a day. You don't need to identify 58 action items and implement them by tomorrow. The great news about having a daily scribing (aka journaling) practice means that you can capture everything. Then, one or two at a time, add them to your success arsenal until they become habits.

What Do You Need to *Stop* Doing?

By now you've most likely added a few items to start doing. If you're wondering where the time is going to come from, this might be the best step of all. It's time to let go of some of the things you've been doing up until now that don't serve you to make room for the ones that do.

I'm fairly sure there are a number of daily activities you will be relieved to stop doing, thankful to delegate to someone else, or grateful to release.

Why not stop

- eating unhealthy, energy-draining foods that suck the life and motivation out of you?

- working when you're tired and on the weekends and holidays?

- replying to texts and emails instantly?

- answering the phone? Let it go to voicemail and reply when the timing works best for you.

- doing repetitive tasks such as paying the bills, buying groceries several times a week, or even cleaning your house?

Or, if you want to dramatically improve your focus in one simple step, try this easy fix:

Stop responding to buzzes and sounds like a trained seal.

Do you really need to be notified when you receive texts, emails, and social media notifications? Nope, didn't think so. Go into the settings of your phone, tablet and computer and turn all of your notifications OFF.

Technology exists for your benefit, and you can take control of it this very minute. How often you check your phone messages, texts, and email can and should be directed by *you*. Let's face it, we're network marketers, not emergency room physicians. We don't need to be accessible and instantly responding to others 24/7/365. An effective alternative is scheduling times throughout the day to check in on what's happening, what needs your immediate attention, what items can be added to your schedule or master to-do list, and also what can be deleted, ignored, or forgotten.

Your voicemail message can let people know you will check it at noon and 4:00 p.m. daily. If their call is an emergency, they can, and should, text you at the same number. By setting proper expectations around response times, prospects, customers, and team members will never be disappointed when it takes you a few hours to get back to them.

Unwavering Focus is a Habit

Focus is like a muscle that you build over time. And, like a muscle, you need to show up and do the work to make it grow. Cut yourself some slack if you falter, but keep pushing forward. It will get easier. It might take you time to learn to focus, but every day that you try, you'll continue to get better at it. Ultimately, this is about *becoming* someone who focuses, which starts with seeing yourself as such. I recommend that you add a few lines to your affirmations about your commitment to unwavering focus and what you will do each day to develop it.

Most network marketers would be shocked to discover just how little time they spend on truly important activities relevant to business growth each day. Today, or in the next 24 hours, schedule 60 minutes to focus on the *single most important business growth task you do*, and you'll be amazed not only by your productivity, but also by how empowering it feels.

By now, you've added some pretty incredible action items and focus areas to your success arsenal. After you complete the steps below, head into the next section where we will sharpen your network marketing skills and combine them with the Life S.A.V.E.R.S. in ways you might not have heard or thought of before!

Your Sales Accelerator Steps

Step One: Free your mind with a brain dump. Unload all those little to-do lists floating around in your head. Create a master to-do list in your journal.

Step Two: Build your Three Unwavering Focus lists:

- **What I need to keep doing (or do more of)**
- **What I need to start doing**

- **What I need to stop doing**

Step Three: For the next week, keep a list of all the things you spend time doing and how long you spend on each task. What can be automated, outsourced, or delegated? How much time did you spend on your top business growth and income-producing activities? Repeat this process until you are clear on what your process is, and start time-blocking your days so that you're spending close to 80 percent of your time on tasks that produce results. Delegate the rest.

Finally, remember to start implementing Hal's not-so-obvious secret to success: *Commit to your process without being emotionally attached to your results.*

TOP ONE PERCENT NETWORKER INTERVIEW

Tanya Aliza

www.TanyaAliza.com

Facebook.com/TanyaAliza

In 2009, Tanya read *The Four Hour Workweek* by Tim Ferriss and it changed everything for her.

Network Marketing found her. She had a girlfriend call her up and invite Tanya to her house for a business presentation. At this presentation the average income was talked about and the presenter stated they were making $350,000 a year and it took them 3 years to get there - Tanya grabbed the application!

In 2010, Tanya got a call that her dad had a stroke and passed away that Sunday. While she was taking time off or work to be with her family, she realized that she still had money coming in from her Network Marketing Business and that was the exact moment she understood residual income

She retired from her finance job in June of 2010 and began learning how to take her business online in late 2010 so that she could move to Costa Rica and continue to build her business in paradise.

In 2013, she became the proud recipient of the "Expert of Experts" award. She's a personal branding specialist that loves helping people generate leads and make sales online. She's had many multi-six-figure product launches and now loves teaching others how to do the same.

Tanya's Miracle Morning & Daily Rituals:

- 7:00 AM - Wake up and have a healthy breakfast while reading a good book.
- 7:30 - Write a blog post and do a little online marketing.

- 9:00 - Gym or Yoga Class.
- 10:30 - Meditation.
- 11:00 - Shower and get ready for the day.

BONUS INTERVIEW FOR *MIRACLE MORNING FOR NETWORK MARKETING* READERS

Each of the Top One Percent Networkers that are featured in this book were interviewed by Pat Petrini about not only their morning routines, but their tips, techniques and strategies that have been critical in helping them become the best of the best in network marketing.

For your free and exclusive interview with Tanya, go to www.TMMforNetworkMarketers.com/Tanya

TOP ONE PERCENT NETWORKER INTERVIEW

Jennifer Glacken

www.GlackenHealth.com

Facebook.com/jenniferglacken

Facebook.com/glackenhw

Twitter.com/jenniferglacken

Pinterest.com/glackenhealth/

After graduating from the University of Virginia in 1988 with a degree in Foreign Affairs and Spanish, Jennifer started my first job as a Sears Executive Management Trainee.

In 1992, her son David was born and Jennifer was introduced to some network marketing products due to some health issues her son had.

She was a customer for 6½ years before deciding in 2000 to build the business after her husband was laid off from his job.

A few of Jennifer's accomplishments:

- Founder of Glacken University

- One of the first people in her company to reach the rank of Senior Master Coordinator (minimum of $2.4 million in sales/year).

- Achieved Top Recruiter in her company in 2011

- 1 of 8 women in Barrington, IL to be nominated for the Athena Leadership Award

- Top Achiever in her company for 2011, 2012, 2013 & 2014

- Wall of Honor for 2011, 2012, 2013 & 2014

Jennifer's Miracle Morning & Daily Rituals:

• 6:00 a.m. - Wake up

• Drink 8oz of warm water with a slice of lemon

- Hydrate with 32oz of water
- Bible Study
- Spend 15 minutes in solitude/meditation/thought about the day
- Go through my affirmations and visualization
- Workout (Bikram Yoga 3-4x/week, personal trainer 3x/week)
- Smoothie and Vitamins
- Read/respond to urgent emails
- Either plan the day or review the plan for the day (done the previous night)
- 8:30 a.m. - Showered and ready for the day

BONUS INTERVIEW FOR *MIRACLE MORNING FOR NETWORK MARKETING* READERS

Each of the Top One Percent Networkers that are featured in this book were interviewed by Pat Petrini about not only their morning routines, but their tips, techniques and strategies that have been critical in helping them become the best of the best in network marketing.

For your free and exclusive interview with Jennifer, go to www.TMMforNetworkMarketers.com/Jennifer

SECTION 2

THE REST OF YOUR DAY AS A NETWORK MARKETER

"Filling out an application doesn't make you a network marketer any more than standing in a garage makes you a car."
—BOB SCHMIDT, Network Marketing Professional

You are now armed with the skills to start out every day feeling amazing and primed to have a productive, fantastic day in your networking marketing business. You have just read and understand how to apply the Life S.A.V.E.R.S., but it still begs the question, what do I do with the rest of my day?

The rest of your day, and the skills you will need to effectively and efficiently grow your network marketing business, are exactly what this section is going to cover: the significant activities to focus your energies on to make sure that, on top of having a Miracle Morning, you make every day as productive and prosperous as possible.

In preparation for this book, I interviewed dozens of the top earners around the world and confirmed what I had discovered in my own experience with network marketing: there are core principles, skills, and strategies you would be wise to layer on top of your Miracle Morning. And you're in luck—I'm going to share them with you!

But before I dive into the specific skills you must master, there are some additional mindset nuances you need to be aware of and adopt as early in your career as you possibly can. Like, now.

Principles Versus Tactics

I'm going to cover principles more than tactics. You might be wondering, what's the difference? Principles are things that apply anywhere and anytime. They are timeless and tend to be a bit more conceptual. Tactics are the details, the execution that brings it all together and creates the tangible results you want.

By way of illustration, more than a decade ago, product and opportunity cassette tapes were a popular tool in network marketing. Over time, tapes became CDs, CDs became DVDs, and DVDs became online videos. The principle is the importance of using presentation tools for third-party credibility. The tactic is the form that the tool might take or precisely what you might say to get the tool in front of the prospect.

I'm not going to focus on tactics as much in this section because the best tactics are going to be specific to your team and company. You'll want to use the same tactics that your team uses so that everybody replicates the same system, which allows your team to more easily duplicate and grow faster.

I'm going to primarily share with you the principles that work no matter what company you're in, no matter where you are in the world, and no matter when you might be reading this book.

Learning to Tie Your Shoes

Have you ever wondered why almost everyone knows how tie their shoes? It may seem like a weird question, but if you are like most people, you know how to tie only one knot, and that is the one you use to tie your shoes. Why does nearly every person know how to do this by the time they are in grade school? The reason is *social pressure*.

There is tremendous social pressure to learn to do the things that everybody else can do. If for some reason you haven't mastered any or all of those skills in what could be considered a normal amount of time, you will be considered an outcast at some level.

The skills required to be an entrepreneur or to build a network marketing business, however, are not normal. Why would they be? Most people spend their entire adult lives working for other people, not building a business.

Prior to joining an organization, we typically don't learn the basic skills needed in network marketing, such as prospecting (finding new people to talk to), presenting (sharing great information), following up (staying in touch), and leading a team.

Because most people don't have these skills, they think that those who are in network marketing who have developed them are unusual in some way. Then we see the social pressure reversed ... there is social pressure to *fail*. When a new person joins our business, they experience social pressure from friends and family, especially those who haven't become successful in businesses of their own, to fail in their endeavor.

It's not so much that they want you to fail. It's that they want you to be like them. Their life and choices feel right to them. So they think you should make the same choices they did.

This is often referred to as "crab mentality." Theoretically, if you put one crab in a bucket and it has the opportunity to escape, it will escape. However, if you put multiple crabs in that same bucket, the one trying to escape will be pulled back in by the others, and not one will be able to escape. While I can't confirm that crabs actually do this, I can tell you *for sure* that humans do.

So, to succeed in network marketing, not only do you need to learn the fundamental skills we cover in this book, you also have to overcome tremendous negative social pressure and be okay with becoming an outcast in many ways.

No social pressure exists for you to become financially independent, start your own home-based business, or become your own boss, but there is tremendous social pressure to *not* do that. Anyone who hasn't created financial independence for themselves (especially those who would like to yet are afraid), secretly (or not so secretly) wants you to fail. Your failure would be validation of their choices and that trying is futile. *But what if you actually succeeded?*

There are other big questions: how do you overcome these obstacles? How do you know if you are strong enough? You know you want to be successful in network marketing, but do you want it badly enough? The answer is: you're going to find out. Maybe it's going to take you six months, a year, maybe even a couple of years. But you're going to find out, because you're either going to make it or you're going to quit.

I don't want you to quit!

You should not quit! *Please do not quit.* You must keep moving toward your network marketing goals, and here's why: there are millions of people around the world, in all different countries, of all different ages, backgrounds, ethnicities, and levels of education who have made tremendous incomes, changed their lives, and built huge businesses, *all in network marketing.* So I ask you to consider this question: Do you honestly believe that there is anything that millions of people can do that you can't also do? I don't think so. And, I hope that you don't either.

Please reread, highlight, and double-underline the paragraph above. Come back and read it any time and every time you need a few words of encouragement.

It's my hope that you don't buy into or accept perceived limitations that you think you have and instead accept and internalize the fact that there are millions of people who have done this, and you can absolutely do it too. Success is just a matter of figuring out, learning, and mastering the right skills.

How do you overcome the social pressure that stands between you and your success in network marketing? Well, the answer to that is to surround yourself with people who are pulling you up, not people who pull you down. Surround yourself with people who practice the Life S.A.V.E.R.S., other beginning business builders, and other successful network marketers. Your new community must consist of those who are talking the same talk and walking the same walk. Their energy and enthusiasm will fuel yours; their success will encourage yours.

I know that "surround yourself with successful people" has almost become cliché. Jim Rohn is often quoted as saying, "You're the average of the five people that you hang out with most." But he wasn't, *isn't*, wrong! This formula for success (or failure) applies to your relationships, your income, your attitude, and even your overall happiness. Almost every aspect of you will likely be the de-termined by the averages of the people you hang out with. It's a cliché because it's true.

To make a real, noticeable change in your life, to grow your business to where you want it to be, you must ensure that you no longer have crabs pulling you down. In their place, you must gather peers and mentors that raise bar of what is normal. You must take an honest look at who you spend most of your time with, and make sure they are the right kinds of people. Your upline, downline, and friends must be handpicked by you to give you the advantage of a powerful support system.

If, for now, you are short on positive, fantastic peers and men-tors, you might want to listen to great podcasts and read self-help and network marketing books (like this one!). Make sure that you put effort into building your online and offline support system be-cause it won't magically happen. Join The Miracle Morning Com-munity on Facebook, find a Miracle Morning accountability part-ner, and make darn sure that every single person in your downline and upline reads this book (shameless, I know, yet my point is still valid!). The more positive social pressure you have to succeed, the better.

Know that your weekly or monthly opportunity and product meetings as part of your network marketing business education are probably not enough to create the daily social pressure that you need. You must develop a daily habit of hanging out with positive people and taking in positive information in addition to what your upline and company provide.

Bonus tip: When you surround yourself with people for whom success is the norm, you will actually accelerate your own success. You'll see other people, who are just like you—only further along the path, achieving success and abundance. Being around them, watching what they do and how they do it, will inspire and encourage you. Surround yourself with people who believe that success in business (and in life) is as expected as learning to tie your shoes. Their level of expectation will become your level of expectation. *That* type of social pressure will push you to success.

Advantages and Disadvantages ... Do Not Exist

I joined my first network marketing company when I was 22 years old, and you can probably guess my first mental block was my age. I felt like I didn't have a lot of credibility when I was talking with people. I was also concerned that prospects wouldn't take me seriously when I presented. I worked incredibly hard, and eventually what seemed to be a weakness actually became one of my biggest strengths. As soon as I started making a little bit of money (from a thousand to a few thousand dollars per month) and I was able to show my success, people who were ten, twenty, or even forty years older than me were thinking, *Well geez, if this punk kid can do it, then I can definitely do it.* My prior disadvantage actually came to work in my favor. But I had to identify the mental block and do the work to get past it before it started working for me.

Take a second and think of a perceived disadvantage that you might have in your life right now. Now, consider ways that this perceived disadvantage might work in your favor now or in the future. For bonus points, write down your disadvantage and then start listing potential positive outcomes underneath it.

For example, let's say you are a single parent. Some people might call that a disadvantage because your time and resources might be more limited than a married parent. But what are the positives of being a single parent? Can you relate to other single parents better? Are you more driven to succeed because of the challenging situation you find yourself in? Is being a single parent better than being married to a crappy spouse?

I'm telling you, when you find a way to overcome that obstacle, there are infinite opportunities within it. Like my friend, Honorée Corder, you could write a book on how you succeeded as a single parent. The people you'll motivate, the people you'll inspire, and the value you'll provide to your team—which are incalculable at this time—will all happen because you overcame those obstacles and became an example of what is possible.

If I paid you $100 for every advantage that you can think of associated with your perceived disadvantage, how many do you think you could come up with? I bet your list would be limited only by the number of $100 bills I have to give you!

Let's say you did write a book about how you overcame your current challenge. How much income might that book bring in? One dollar? Ten million dollars? Anything in between? What advantages might those extra dollars open up? What about the recognition you might get from the book? Who might you meet because of it and what new doors may open as a result? What are the many possible advantages that could splinter from any of those possible outcomes? Do you see how long this list can get?

My goal is for you to realize that there are an infinite number of positive outcomes directly linked to your current perceived disadvantage. That is not hyperbole. The precise number is infinite. And guess what? Every one of those advantages has an infinite number of disadvantages linked to it. Sure, you could write the book on succeeding as a single mom, but do you know what sucks about that …writing the book! (As a side note: writing doesn't come particularly easy to me.)

If every situation has an infinite number of potentially positive outcomes and an infinite number of potentially negative outcomes, then the positives and negatives cancel out and we are left with the conclusion that every situation is neutral. The stress that we feel when we are in a seemingly tough situation is a result of the outcomes that we choose to focus on, not the reality of the situation.

I can't stress enough that this is not positive thinking; it's physics. Advantages and disadvantages only exist in your head.

Young people have energy. Old people have wisdom. Big companies have resources. Small companies have agility. Non-parents have time. Parents have motivation. Established companies have stability. Startups have massive upside. And on and on.

To me, this is what truly makes us all equal as human beings. It doesn't matter where you come from, how much money you have, or what you want to accomplish. You have an infinite number of factors helping you to achieve your goals and an infinite number of factors working against you. You choose which ones you want to give power to.

Here is an actual excerpt of my Miracle Morning affirmations that I remind myself of every morning. Feel free to use it or modify it if you think it might help you:

"Advantages and disadvantages are false constructs. They don't exist. Therefore, frustration, anxiety, and stress are irrational reactions to what are actually neutral situations. Nothing is 'good' or 'bad,' it just is. And, why would it make sense to stress about something that is? I choose to focus on what I can control and accept situations for what they are. Things will never be better, nor will they ever be worse. I choose to be happy at this moment."

Nick Vujicic has several videos on YouTube you'll want to see. He was born with no arms and no legs, but today he's a successful entrepreneur, speaker, author, and investor. He's a really amazing guy and a true inspiration, but you could look at him and say, "Man, there's no way he can achieve success—he has too many chips stacked against him."

Nick is the first to say, "I was born with no arms and no legs. What an amazing disadvantage, right? No way!" According to Nick, not only has he succeeded in spite of his seeming disadvantage, but he is who he is today *because* he was born with no arms or legs. Such a massive obstacle is actually what created the opportunity for him to succeed. It gave him the opportunity to overcome, which led to the many opportunities and the success that he has today.

Some people have a really hard time with this because it robs them of the story that they've been telling themselves, their rationalization for why it is okay that they haven't succeeded (whatever that means to them). Don't be one of those people. You have exactly as many advantages and disadvantages as every other human … zero.

I recommend you completely abandon the idea that you have disadvantages and instead look at your obstacles as opportunities. Your obstacles provide the direction you've got to go: *through them.* They are your roadmap! Once you figure out a way to overcome them, your real opportunity lies on the other side.

How many appointments are on your calendar?

When I got started in network marketing, I had the great fortune to find a seasoned, well-respected mentor with decades of industry experience and billions of dollars in sales under his belt. His name was Bob, and Bob could be an abrasive and intimidating guy. He was actually a big softy, but most people never got to see that side of him. Most people saw a guy who thought like an engineer, was built like a boxer, had made many millions of dollars in his career, and had zero patience for excuses or complaining. And, he didn't hesitate to call you out! He had a knack for making people nervous and pissing people off.

Bob would allow me to listen in on training calls or strategy sessions with other business builders. Sometimes they were for the leader of another group, and other times a new person who was just getting started on Bob's team. I wanted to listen to soak up and internalize as much of his knowledge as I possibly could. And, of course, I wanted to apply his teachings and advice to myself and my business.

More often than not, the person he was speaking to would say something like, "I'm really struggling. I'm having challenges, and I'm not hitting my goals. I'm not moving as fast as I want to." At first I thought he would share some mystical secret or sage advice or maybe some key phrases that would turn any newbie into a masterful recruiter. Instead, it was usually advice that was so stupid-simple that the recipient might feel like an idiot for not knowing it. In fact, that's usually how the call ended ... with the person feeling a bit like an idiot because they knew he was right.

Bob's calls would almost always begin the same way, with the person thanking him for his time, and then diving into their questions. I always loved listening to his response, and I didn't have to listen in on many calls before I realized they would all end the same way. He would say, "Woah, woah, woah! Hold on a second. Before we start digging into some of your questions, let me ask you a couple of my questions."

Then, he'd ask, "Do you have your calendar with you?"

Today our calendars are right in our phones, but at that time, most people had paper calendars. Regardless, Bob would go on. He'd say, "Go ahead and pull out your calendar for me, and let's turn it to next week." Then the key phrase, "I want you to count up how many appointments you have on your calendar related to your business for next week." Dead silence. Very uncomfortable dead silence.

You could feel their pain as the answer came out of their mouth. "Zero" or "one" or maybe "I've got two!" Bob would continue, "Let me ask you this: if you were a dentist and you had zero (or two) appointments on your calendar for next week, how long would you think you're going to stay in business?" Or, he would say, "If you owned a hair salon and you opened your calendar to next week and you had zero appointments on the calendar, how long do you think that salon would stay in business?"

You're a network marketer. If you have zero appointments on your calendar for next week, how long do *you* expect to stay in business?

As I'm sure you understand, the point was immediately very clear to the people Bob was talking to ... and that was usually the end of the strategy session.

The Four Appointments

It makes sense that to build a large, successful network marketing business, you have to have appointments on your calendar. But it begs the question: *What appointments should be on the calendar?* I'm going to cover the four types of appointments you should have on your calendar each week, and then in subsequent chapters I will dive into the actual skills associated with them. These skills are the fundamental skills that will unlock success for you in network marketing.

I will cover each of these in detail in the chapters that follow, but here's a sneak preview:

Number One: Prospecting. This can be almost anything that puts you in touch with new people who may be great prospects. Online, this might be through social media or running marketing campaigns that drive people into your sales funnel. Offline, it might mean that you are at events, trade shows, or just engaging people that you encounter in your everyday life. Bottom line, you are reaching out in some way and contacting potential new prospects.

Number Two: Presenting. You've prospected, and now you have to introduce these prospects to a presentation. In other words, you actually share the story with those new prospects. In your presentation appointments, you introduce your products or your business opportunity—or maybe both, depending upon the situation.

Number Three: Following Up. Following up is touching base with anyone you have presented to. You want to build the relationship with them, and gauge their readiness to become a customer or join your team. Together, you both decide what the next step is.

Number Four: Getting Started Sessions. The final and probably most important appointments to have on your calendar are the getting started sessions. You want every person who joins your business to have a clear path to early success, and in these sessions, each brand new marketer learns exactly what to do to get their business started *right now.*

Think of it this way: these four appointments are the only action items that build your business and make you money. *Everything else is busy work.* Education like listening to or reading great books is important. Podcasts are fantastic, and filling your mind with good material is critical. Doing the Life S.A.V.E.R.S. sets you up to have a great day every day. But none of that is going to build the business for you or make you any money; you've got to take action. Ensuring that your calendar is full of these four appointments every single week will be the difference between hitting your goals ... or joining the ever-growing list of people who have failed in network marketing!

Note: I'd highly recommend picking up the book *Mastery* by Robert Greene (yes, I recommended it in an earlier chapter ... It's that good!). It is one of the best books I've ever read. It gives you the formula for becoming a true master of any skill or subject matter of your choice. If you apply that formula to the skills in this book, you'll be unstoppable as a network marketing professional.

We just have one more step before we dive into the four appointments and the skills they require. First, we need to take an honest look at your calendar using the *Wealth Formula* and clear some room so that we can pack as many of these appointments into your calendar as possible.

The Wealth Formula

I learned the *Wealth Formula* from one of my long-time friends and mentors, Cindy Samuelson, who is also one of the featured contributors of this book. Be sure to check out her interview just before the next chapter.

I love sharing it because it really surprises people. It's almost like a slap in the face when you hear it for the first time, and it really makes you take an honest look at how you spend your time.

The whole idea of the Wealth Formula is that we're all equal in the sense that we each have 24 hours every day. The difference between where we are now and where we are one year from now or five years from now is how we spend that time.

Now, if you ask people how many hours there are in a week, most wouldn't be able to tell you, let alone tell you how they spend them.

So, let's go ahead and break it down:

24 hours per day x 7 days per week = 168 hours per week TO-TAL

Of course, there are a few needs that most people spend some time on. For example, we need to sleep (unfortunately!). I've tried to fight that all my life, but we do have to sleep.

8 hours per day to sleep x 7 days per week = 56 hours per week for sleep.

I know. Most people wish they could sleep eight hours a day. But let's go ahead and use 8 hours anyway for illustration purposes.

Next, we need to pay the bills (work). If we're not already financially independent in some way, we've got to work a job while we're working on our dream, whatever that might be. So, most people probably need 40 hours per week for that.

8 hours per day to work x 5 days per week = 40 hours per week to work.

You might be thinking, *I wish I worked 40 hours a week. I work WAY more than that.* Well, if you're working way more than 40 hours a week on a job you don't love, then you might want to do something about that. Is there another job that might allow you to pay the bills on 40 hours per week or less that you could switch to soon? Is your current job truly requiring more than 40 hours per week, or are you allowing the job to consume that extra time? Regardless, it might be a good time to read *The 4 Hour Workweek* by Tim Ferriss! That book truly changed my life.

Lastly, we need to have some free time for recreation, friends, family and things like that. Let's give you 6 hours per day to do that.

WHAT?! There's no way I get 6 hours a day of free time to spend with family! I know. We're going to address that. Let's just jot that down for now and I'll explain more momentarily.

6 hours per day free time x 7 days per week = 42 hours per week free time.

So...

- 168 hours per week TOTAL
- 56 hours per week for sleep
- 40 hours per week to pay the bills
- 42 hours per week free time
- = 30 hours per week remaining! [*GASP*]

It makes you wonder ... Where does all that time go?

For many of us, we whittle it away on things that don't bring value to our lives. A daily commute can suck up 20 hours per week for some people and the simple act of eating can consume even more time! Is it possible to convert some of these activities from wasted time into valuable time? Of course it is! Your daily commute is an opportunity to be consuming great audiobooks and podcasts that inspire and inform. It can also be a fantastic time to (safely) spend on the phone connecting with prospects and team members and growing your business! The same applies to eating. Lunch time could be a great time to learn or spend on the phone while dinner can be extremely valuable time with family or friends.

"But, my circumstances are different. I don't have as much time as other people."

Yes, you do. You have 24 hours per day, just like everybody else. And how you spend every minute of those 24 for hours is entirely up to you. Remember earlier on when we discussed the importance of taking 100% responsibility for your life? That applies to your calendar just like it applies to everything else. It is important for each of us to recognize that every minute of our day is spent on activities of our own choosing. Yes, every single minute. We say things like "I *have* to do this" but that is a little lie that we tell ourselves. We each have an infinite numbers of things we can be doing at any moment. Whatever we *choose* to do in that moment is a choice to *not* do everything else.

Most of us run from crisis to crisis, and we don't really manage our time. We don't discipline and defend our time, so it gets wasted on little things and other people's emergencies, and then we have no time for ourselves. If you choose to follow the *Wealth Formula*, then your first step might be to take control of your allotted free time. Manage it in a way that you are squeezing every drop of value from it. It truly is possible to get a full night's sleep, pay the bills, have plenty of recreation time and *still* have 30 hours a week leftover!

So what should you do with your new-found 30 hours?

Cindy Samuelson would say that you want to spend an hour a day "sharpening your saw." Meaning, put good stuff into your head by reading great books (this could be your commute!). I would add listening to great podcasts to that category as I've recently become a bit of a podcast junkie.

Given that you are currently reading *The Miracle Morning for Network Marketers*, an hour per day could also be devoted to incorporating your Miracle Morning, which might include your daily reading/listening time as part of it. However much time to want to devote is obviously up to you.

What I think is amazing is that even when you spend one hour per day on your Miracle Morning, that *still* leaves you with 23 hours left in the week! And, it's how you spend those 23 hours that is really going to fill the gap between where you are today and where you want to be a year or five years down the road. It's the relationships you build. It's the phone calls you make. It's the appointments you set and the sales you close using those 23 hours that build your business, build your dream, or achieve whatever it is that you're trying to accomplish.

TOP ONE PERCENT NETWORKER INTERVIEW

Cindy Samuelson

http://www.cindysamuelson.com

http://www.facebook.com/cindy.samuelson1

http://www.twitter.com/cindysam2002

https://www.linkedin.com/pub/cindy-samuelson

My mom was a single parent of five and I was the oldest. I went to work at 17, graduated from high school at 18, and managed to get about 80 hours of college credit before personal circumstances took my attention away from completing my education. Quitting school was a decision I regretted well into my 40's.

Even as a teen, I knew something for certain. To honor all the sacrifices my mother made for us, I wanted to be *happily married;* I wanted to *stay home and raise my children;* I wanted to *be wealthy.*

I started my home-based business in 1983. Being a great student, I got trained by some of the greatest icons in the industry. I learned early on to make my priorities, "God, first, Family, second, and Career, third … *not thirty-third."* I earned my first million before my 40th birthday … and my second by my 42nd.

It's been a career which has now entered its fourth decade. I've always said I'd never tire of what I do and, here I am, *still passionate.* Still believing if everyone knew what I knew about networking, they'd run, open armed, into their glorious future.

For me networking is about leadership, compassion, and being part of the solution. It's about hope, discipline, persistence and a willingness to show up. It's about learning the skill sets to discipline your disappointments and to encourage yourself to move forward in your darkest hours. It's about learning to be the best version of yourself and to put others needs before your own.

I've been featured in books and magazines. Interviewed by Pulitzer Prize winning authors. I've received standing ovations from rooms filled with 10,000 networkers. More than 45 families have earned more than a million dollars as a result of my involvement in networking. I never get tired of applauding their success.

From owners to distributors, I've met some of the best in the business. That said, I'm to the point in my career where I have no desire to list my credentials. All the titles and awards are no longer what drives me. Though I always have a professional financial objective, my only focus is to help others. I have no desire to do anything more than help others develop the skill sets to live life on their terms. So ... in conclusion ... I think the next 20 years will be the most rewarding of my career.

Cindy's Miracle Morning & Daily Rituals:

- I start my day by ending it well. After my 40th birthday, I became fastidious about removing makeup, exfoliating and moisturizing *(I wish I'd developed the habit in my teens!)*. But more than my skin, I'm maniacal about brushing and flossing my teeth *(simply because dental health is paramount to overall wellness!)*. I work to be in bed close to the same time every night *(I miss my 10:30 window more than I'd like to admit, but I give it my best)*. I'm well rested with 6.5 hours sleep and overly tired with 8.5. For the last 25 years our bedroom has had no TV or phone *(our cell phones, with ringers off, charge overnight in our office)*. I think our bedroom is for private conversations with my husband, intimacy, and sleep.

- I wake up before dawn without the use of an alarm clock. I'm definitely a lark by nature and am happiest in the morning. I've also learned it's hard to fail my family if I'm willing to start my day at 4 am.

- I take my supplements first thing and follow it with a light, protein rich breakfast within my first 90 minutes. A hard boiled egg and a piece of fresh fruit is perfect.

- Being a communicator, I read and write for a minimum of one hour each morning.

- I'm goal driven and have had written goals since 1990. I review my goals and goal statement which are written and carried in my ever present At-a-Glance calendar.

- Not religious, I do a combination of prayer, meditation and gratitude time. In the last couple of years I've found myself reverting to disciplines from my childhood *(another way of saying I often find myself on my knees, head bowed)*.

- I do something physical. Housework, walking, hiking, riding my bike. My Jawbone, which I've worn since May, 2014, is my best reminder to get in 10,000 steps a day.

- At 7:30 I'm ready to brush my teeth, shower, do my makeup, and dress.

- I'm at work at 8:30am.

BONUS INTERVIEW FOR MIRACLE MORNING READERS

Each of the Top One Percent Networkers that are featured in this book were interviewed by Pat Petrini about not only their morning routines, but their tips, techniques and strategies that have been critical in helping them become the best of the best in network marketing.

For your free and exclusive interview with Cindy, go to www. TMMforNetworkMarketers.com/Cindy

TOP ONE PERCENT NETWORKER INTERVIEW

Keala Kanae

www.KealaKanae.com

Facebook.com/keala.kanae

Keala was introduced to network marketing at the age of 18 and quickly swore off the industry just two months later.

He went on to graduate with a BA in Psychology in 2006 from the University of Hawaii but failed for 11 years as an entrepreneur.

In 2012, he returned to network marketing while earning minimum wage at a coffee shop.

A Few of Keala's Accomplishments:

- First 5-figure month within 7 months of returning to network marketing.

- Invited to speak at multiple events to crowds of thousands.

- Ranked within the top 0.00025% of his first full-time NM company with over 200,000 reps.- Has groomed four 6-figure earners and many more full-time networkers.

- Spearheaded the development of an online sales funnel that is currently generating 6-figures per month in sales for his team and has ranked them #1 in production with his company.

- An in-demand trainer on the topics of online lead generation, Facebook ads, and hypnotic selling & persuasion.

- Recently launched his own coaching product which grossed over $130,000 in sales in its first 30 days.

- His greatest pleasure is teaching and training network marketers how to duplicate the online sales processes that he's used to generate over $1 million in gross sales in just 2 years.

Keala's Miracle Morning & Daily Rituals:

- Read - entrepreneurism/personal development/influence (minimum of 30 minutes)
- Morning Affirmations (5 minutes)
- Practice Gratitude (5 minutes)
- Meditation/Silence (5-10 mins)
- I also listen to audio programs daily but not necessarily in the morning

BONUS INTERVIEW FOR *MIRACLE MORNING FOR NETWORK MARKETING* READERS

Each of the Top One Percent Networkers that are featured in this book were interviewed by Pat Petrini about not only their morning routines, but their tips, techniques and strategies that have been critical in helping them become the best of the best in network marketing.

For your free and exclusive interview with Keala, go to www. TMMforNetworkMarketers.com/Keala

PURPOSEFUL PROSPECTING

"Whenever you find yourself on the side of the majority, it is time to pause and reflect."
–MARK TWAIN, Classic American Author and Humorist

Each of the four appointments I discussed in the previous chapter is crucial for any network marketer's success; however, at the top of the list is prospecting. Purposeful prospecting is the first skill you must master to become a superior network marketer.

Prospecting is a broad topic because it can be done in a lot of different ways; there are countless options for prospecting both online and offline. Most network marketing leaders today are doing a healthy amount of both.

A prospect is defined as a "potential or likely customer or marketer." Fundamentally, the act of prospecting is nothing more complicated than reaching out to new people who are potential customers of your products, and/or marketers for your business, and inviting them to take a look at your offerings.

It sounds simple, right? Actually, it is.

Where Are the People?

People are everywhere! There are people out there killing it with online prospecting strategies by running ads to drive traffic into their online marketing funnels—this is a fantastic method of online prospecting. Others, who don't consider themselves tech-savvy, prefer offline prospecting by meeting people as they are out in the world. You can meet great people at coffee shops, grocery stores, on airplanes and in airports, and at trade shows. There are even a few who find huge success with direct mail campaigns.

How can you craft a strategy that works for you? Follow the model of other successful network marketers. Find a mentor whose personality is most like yours. You don't have to reinvent the wheel—you simply take a page from their book of effective actions. Ideally, find someone within your company. In fact, the opportunity to work with a particular successful leader might be a good reason to join a particular company in the first place.

Where Do I find People?

The simple answer to this question is to live a good life. What does that mean? It means that your best and most sustainable prospecting strategy is to get out in the world and live an exciting and happy life. Make a point of meeting lots of people as you go, and I promise you are never (ever!) going to run out of people to connect with or talk to. A happy, excited person is a magnet for excellent people—and excellent people are exactly who you want to find. Ultimately, this is a strategy anyone and everyone can execute, including you.

This is what I suggest to new marketers on my team: sit down and make a list of things you've always wanted to do. What are things you've always wanted to learn, and do? Where are the places you've always wanted to go? Maybe you've always wanted to learn Jujitsu. That's awesome—Jujitsu is very popular, and you'll most likely meet lots of interesting people. Find a local *ryu* (school), sign up for weekly classes, and of course meet all the people in your class. If you've always wanted to learn a second language, sign up for classes at your local community college or language school. You might want to lead a study group. If you've always wanted to go back to school and get a degree, perhaps your MBA, sweet. Go and do night classes, and again form or join a study group. If you've always wanted to become a skydiver, start going skydiving on the weekends. You love scrapbooking? Join a scrapbooking group.

A great resource for finding all kinds of groups in your area is Meetup.com. You'll find virtually an unlimited number of specialty groups you can join. If you want to talk politics, there are political groups you can join. You want to get in shape? Join a running club, or take a regular spin class. You've always wanted to travel? Pick a *National Geographic* tour and see the world. Guess who will be with you? Lots and lots of other cool people with similar interests to yours.

Each of these activities are going to enrich your life and open doors. Along the way, you'll be meeting other people that may be great candidates as customers or marketers for your business.

The Secret Sauce

Your secret sauce in prospecting is going to be the unshakable, indefatigable positive attitude you develop through your use of the Life S.A.V.E.R.S.

Crafting affirmations about meeting people everywhere you go who are interested in joining your team, attracting the right people to you who sign up and purchase lots of products, even getting, and being in the best shape of your life … all of these will contribute to your success. Your inner personal growth will directly influence the outer growth you experience in your business.

Imagine your entire team—company!—practicing the Life S.A.V.E.R.S. How cool would it be to have team-wide affirmations? What about providing a visualization to your team that helps them visualize the activities necessary for earning the annual trip or a fully-loaded bonus car? Pretty cool, right?

Sales? Really?

As you are prospecting, you might be worried about the word *sales*, being a salesperson, or even being perceived as a salesperson. The mental image conjured when the word salesperson is used is often a sleazy car salesperson, complete with slicked-back hair and cheesy tactics. Perhaps you've been shopping for a car, and a salesperson got you into the office and then brought in the closer to pressure you into signing the contract. If this is what you picture when you think of sales, consider this: Those are examples of sales done wrong.

We can agree those are un-enjoyable and ineffective sales situations. In those situations, you most likely did not buy, or if you did, you came out of it wondering if you made the right decision. Let's talk about sales and selling done right. (You can even read *The Miracle Morning for Salespeople* if you want to truly master the art of selling, Miracle Morning-style.)

Keep this in mind as you are prospecting for customers and marketers alike: your job is to combine your knowledge of your product, service, or opportunity with the prospect's knowledge of their life, wants, and needs to *help them* decide if they would benefit by what you have to offer. *This* is selling done correctly.

Helping people to make the right buying decision *for them* is selling done right. As a marketer and representative of your company, opportunity, and products, you are helping each person to make a decision that will make their life better, even if that means they say no to what you have to offer.

You'll know you are truly being a good salesperson when you turn people away because they are not a great fit for your business or products. You are looking for those who can benefit most from what you have to offer (from the products or business). Your job is to educate them and help them make their best decision. That is sales done right!

Network Marketing Is a Numbers Game—You Have to Play to Win!

It is way more fun to have a lot of plates in the air (so to speak), than to have just one person on your prospect list. If you've only got one person that you're working on, then you *need* that person to say yes! Your whole world revolves around their saying yes. If they do, you'll be on top of the world, if they don't, it's a bad, bad day (and tomorrow won't be great, either). When you have just one person on your calendar, then you are nervous about how that appointment is going to go. That's too much pressure to have on that one prospect, and *waaaay* too much pressure to have on yourself!

The alternative to the stressful "they must say yes" scenario is to have 15 or 20, or even better 40–50, prospects in the hopper at any given time. With that many people in the follow-up process, when one person says no, you just don't care that much. In fact, you get excited about it, because you're like, "Thank goodness, I can check that person off of my list."

Because you're so spread out, you are also spread thin. You've got all these plates in the air; and it's exciting to be able to check people off so that you can focus on the yes's and the potential yes's. Building your business becomes simultaneously a lot more fun and a lot less stressful. It's exciting to try to keep all the plates in the air, and if some fall through the cracks, that's okay. That's way better than not having that many to choose from in the first place.

The Early "Yes" Makes a Difference

Your first goal is to get a few yes's under your belt as quickly as possible. The early yes's help you feel good, as well as build belief in what you're doing. Those early yes's increase your confidence because they tell you that you are on the right track. You'll want to get some early yes's and help your new marketers to get them too.

When someone new comes into my business, I recommend a strong focus on building sustainable prospecting strategies, while simultaneously urging them to go ahead and talk with nice, supportive friends and family. You want to reach out to your friendlies and say, "Hey, this is something I'm doing. Would you be open to taking a look?" Your closest friends and family are likely the first people to say yes to you and support you. Some of them will call you crazy too, but even they are more likely to do you a favor and look than a stranger is. You get a little bit of practice and a win or two under your belt. These yes's help build your confidence right out the gate.

On the flip side, the last thing you want any new person to do (including yourself) is to approach people they don't know well or to try to sponsor people who intimidate them. Those initial calls can go poorly, and you can get shot down or be unable to answer key questions. Suddenly, you are petrified to pick up the phone. Start with the low hanging fruit (perhaps your family, close friend, or coworkers). With each call and each ask, your skills improve, your confidence rises, and you get better. When that happens, you'll be comfortable going after the bigger wins.

The Invitation

The best prospecting could actually be called *inviting*. A long way from trying to convince or sell someone on our products or opportunity, we're inviting the people we meet, people we *like*, to simply take a look. They could say yes to the opportunity or the products—or both. Or, they might say no—and that's quite okay, too. Your job is to invite them to a presentation (which is the topic I'm going to cover in detail in the next chapter). You invite people to a presentation, whether it's a company meeting, webinar, online video, conference call, three-way call with your sponsor or upline, or even a home party.

Remember though, the invitation is *not* a presentation. The purpose is only to pique their interest enough to get them to the presentation. It should leave them wondering. Don't hit them with a fire-hose of information about how amazing your product or opportunity is. You're likely to quickly turn people off and come off as salesy if your invitation is overpowering. If they have questions, let them know that the presentation will likely answer them. The purpose of the invitation is more about creating questions in their mind instead of answering them.

Extend lots and lots and lots (did I mention *lots?*) of invitations. Don't be too wrapped up in the answer you get. The more no's you get, the more the yes's will pile up over time.

Speaking of numbers …

How Many People Do I Need to Invite?

All of them. Not really, but I got your attention, right? When my new marketers get started, they are excited to begin inviting people to a presentation (which may be online or offline). They will say, "I invited fifteen people and only one, or no one, showed up," and then they say, "Gosh, I guess it's really hard to invite people and get them to show up."

Let me pose a question to you: if you were giving away $100 bills to every person who showed up to your presentation, how many people do you think you could get to show up to that presentation, whatever it might be? I'm sure that your answer is: probably quite a few! You could probably get more than one hundred, maybe even a thousand people there.

So, the question isn't whether you can get people to the presentation. You absolutely *can* get people to the presentation. You just have to make your invitation strong and (ahem) *inviting* enough for them to see the value in attending. The key is to allow the prospect to see the value so they make it a point to show up to the presentation. If you're wondering how to make compelling invitations, find the best person in your company or upline who gets yes's to their invitations, and do exactly what they do,say what they say in the way that they say it and you will get the results that they do.

The Why and the Who

There are a couple of key points to keep in mind when you invite people to check out a presentation. Before you open your mouth, understand why are you talking to this particular person. Why did you invite them to take a look at what you do? I would suggest that your answer should be something other than the fact that they are breathing. The best invitation is an authentic invitation that has been carefully thought out and has their best interest at heart.

Hopefully you are inviting them because you know or may have learned something about them, and you feel that what you have to offer is a good fit for their needs. The only way that you can learn anything about them is if you take the time to ask questions.

For example, you've met somebody in your Spanish study group. You've had a little get-to-know-you time because you've asked them questions, learned about their life, and some of their wants and desires. They may have mentioned what they do now, and what they wish they were doing— perhaps they've mentioned they wish they could make more money or afford a trip to Spain to use their new language. As you ask lots of questions, it's those questions that are going to give you a sort of a roadmap to how to invite them to take a look at what you have.

On the other hand, if you have no reason for inviting this person (other than the fact that they are breathing), they will know instantly you are just looking at them as a dollar sign. They will know you are just one more person trying to get them on your product or into your downline, but not because you actually care about them. People have a spidey-sense, and they will know your true intention, without your ever revealing it. Make sure your intentions are genuine, and your results will astound you.

I can't emphasize this enough. Forget being slick. Forget worrying about the right line that is going to grab them. Be honest. Be open. Be authentic in your communication with people. They may say no, but they will trust you more because they can tell that you're being straight with them. Trust is always more valuable in the long run.

Natural Conversations

There's a funny thing that happens when an individual joins a network marketing company. They fall in love with the products and/or opportunity, but all of the sudden (the minute they are compensated for their endorsement), they lose the ability to talk like a human being and they sound like a walking brochure.

The key is to keep the natural conversation and enthusiasm going, even after the added component of compensation comes into play.

Consider this: when you go see a great movie and you love it, you have no problem bringing it up in conversation and sharing with the next person you see. You see your friend the next day, you talk to him about this great movie you saw, or you might even post about it on Facebook. "Just saw Mission Impossible III. Mind blown! You have to see this movie!" Ever said something like that?

You don't need any training to know how to recommend a fantastic restaurant (Morton's Steakhouse!) or an awesome product that you just tried (do you remember when you first held an iPhone?). Have you ever had a friend make a buying decision because of your recommendation? Was it because you read a book by Robert Cialdini on persuasion and carefully constructed your recommendation to grab their attention? No! You authentically shared your excitement with them, and your authenticity and enthusiasm resonated.

Have you ever recommended a product so effusively that you suddenly stopped and said, "Man, I should be getting paid to talk about this!" Well, now you are. And that could be part of your problem.

To get an example of what I'm talking about, go on social media and look at how other people in network marketing communicate. Most likely, they are doing it terribly. Are their posts grabbing your attention? Piquing your interest? Or pushing you away? Does it feel like they are authentically communicating how their product can help you, or does it feel like they are only interested in making a buck?

Natural conversations are a difficult area for network marketers to master. When someone joins a new business, they seem to lose the ability to naturally communicate with people about the product or service they offer. How do you overcome this? By becoming aware of what works and what doesn't. This concept applies both online and offline, but social media is a great place to learn about this and see it in action. Jump online (try Facebook, it's a great place to start) and watch for people who are sharing or recommending products they have no vested interest in. You might see someone write, "I just took my first Uber. No wonder taxis hate this company! It was awesome!" You might see recommendations for an app that someone loves. Compare those authentic endorsements to the not-so-natural communication that you see. Once you get your antennae up, examples will start jumping out at you everywhere.

- What sort of words are they using?
- What's the difference between what they say that works and what someone else is doing when they are selling in an awkward and ineffective way?
- Notice *why* some sound natural when they are communicating something and others don't and why.

Let me be clear, the goal of natural communication is not to try and mask the fast that you are being paid to represent a product or service. In most cases, that will be obvious. The goal is to prevent the fact that you are getting paid from clouding your ability to properly communicate your legitimate excitement about your product or service, or how it can benefit others. If you can learn to speak naturally about your products or services, and even about your business, then you are going to have entirely different results in the way that people respond to you—both online and offline.

Don't Do Me Any Favors

At the very beginning, when you're going after some easy yes's, you may ask close family and friends to do you a favor and take a look at what you're doing. But this is *not* your long-term strategy. The folks who are closest to you are the lucky few who get to be a part of your practice round. But I want to stress that you aren't looking for people to take pity on you. You aren't desperate, and your prospects are not supposed to pity you or do you a favor.

If you take the pity approach, "Hey, would you please do me the favor of looking at it?" or worse, "Please do me the favor of buying it," you are coming from a place of weakness and not providing a positive experience for your prospects. Remember, you're offering could be exactly what they need, and might be a good fit for them. It is your job to find out. Ultimately, you want each of your prospects to walk away from their encounters with you impressed with desire to identify their needs and help them, even if that doesn't mean buying your product.

The Invitation

So, you're out in the world and you've got a live prospect! (Congratulations!) You're excited because the person you've met has a sparkle in their eye and a spring in their step. You can see yourself working well with them or see your product or service changing their life for the better.

But what do you say? That's the million-dollar question, right?

You will ask your prospect to take a look at your product or service, and, in certain circumstances, to look at the business opportunity as well. Here are three powerful tips for prospecting success:

Tip #1: The Market Research Approach.

Your powerful prospecting question here is, "Hey, I was recently asked to do some marketing for a new company that just came out with X product. We're looking for people to try it and give us their honest feedback. In return, we're offering a full refund to anybody that doesn't love it for any reason. It is really the feedback on the price, the product and the process that is valuable to us. Would you be open to something like that?"

Tip #2: The "You said" Approach.

Earlier I discussed the importance of taking the time to get to know people and ask them questions and how those questions can be a roadmap to your invitation. Well, this is when you get to use that information. "You know, I was thinking about you and how the other day you mentioned money was tight. You shared that you needed to find something you could do from home. Well, I have no idea if it'd be a good fit for you or not, but I've got something that I would love to show you. Would you be open to checking out this presentation with me?" They said they were looking for something, and you are now offering a possible solution. This approach is very comfortable and very natural.

Tip #3: The Sincere Compliment Approach.

This approach is pretty straight-forward. You compliment the prospect and make the ask: "Hey, I've found something that I'm really excited about. I would love for you to take a look at it because [insert sincere compliment], and I thought you might really dig it. It may or may not be a great fit for you, but I'd love for you to take a look." Maybe they are a natural leader or have an amazing mind for business and can see things that others can't; they may be extremely health conscious or are really respected by everybody around them. By authentically complimenting them, you open them up to what you have to say next. In addition, you tell them you recognize what you're sharing might or might not be a good fit, which allows them to say no without the fear of hurting your feelings. Giving them an out drops any tension there might be.

Use Your Life S.A.V.E.R.S.

When you're about to make an invitation, I advise you to visualize the invitation going exceptionally well. In fact, spend a few minutes visualizing the different ways it could go well. Otherwise, it will be easy to sell yourself on the fact the invitation won't go well and maybe convince yourself not to approach the person at all.

You can also incorporate affirmations into your prospecting, such as *"I leave every person I speak to better than I found them because I genuinely care about what is happening in their lives and I'm not afraid to give them an honest compliment. Whether they are a yes or a no, they are glad that they spoke to me!"* Your mindset really does influence your outcome.

Remember, while you are worried about how other people are going to respond to you, they are spending their whole life worried about what the world thinks of them. Prospect or quit. Those are your only options.

Powerful Prospecting with Social Media

I highly recommend you learn to use social media the right way, and right away, because as prospecting tools go, it's incredibly powerful. If your company is opening up a new market, social media gives you the ability to instantly access people in that market *for free*. You can find other powerful strategies that allow you to source nearly unlimited new prospects once you learn how to connect with people online. There are free strategies and paid strategies, and they are all changing very fast, but they are well worth the time to learn.

In fact, social media and network marketing could be the topic of a book in and of itself, or even several. I highly recommend the book *Magnetic Sponsoring: How to Attract Endless Leads and Distributors to You Automatically* by Mike Dillard. It's a phenomenal book that can provide a great starting point for you to learn how to start online prospecting.

Before we jump into presenting, there is one final point I want to make about powerful prospecting: the principles of prospecting, presenting, and recruiting *online* are no different from the principles of prospecting, presenting, and recruiting *offline*. Powerful prospecting is and will always be about the ability meet people, learn what is important to them and to build relationships. You simply have to find the tactics you like, the ones that resonate with and work for you, and perform them consistently and repeatedly until you have built an organization that will fund your dreams.

TOP ONE PERCENT NETWORKER INTERVIEW

Rob Robson

www.RobRobsonBlog.com

Facebook.com/ebizrobson

Twitter: @ebizrobson

At 21 years of age, Rob was able to transition from addiction & depression to financially independent & a professional speaker in just 6 months through completely eliminating all media & immersing himself in personal development books and audios 6 - 10 hours per day.

Rob & his wife Kenyon have achieved the prestigious rank of "Life Coach" in their company. At the time of this writing, the average Life Coach earns $137,441 per month.

The Robsons have 5 children of their own & intend to continue to grow their family by fostering & adopting a "bunch" more.

Rob's Miracle Morning & Daily Rituals:

- My day usually starts between 6-7am, depending on when our first "alarm clock" climbs into our bed to get my attention.

- The first thing I do is grab my phone to quickly remind my slow-to-fire morning synapses of what is on my calendar that day.

- We do our best to start every morning with family prayer & scripture study (sometimes our "best" is a quick prayer just before the kids jump out of the moving car in order beat the school bell!).

- Other than when she is 13 months pregnant or when we have a newborn that doesn't sleep, Kenyon & I love to exercise together in the morning. This can range from a short walk around the block to a trip to the gym depending on our schedule that day.

- I normally walk into my office around 9:30am & before I wake up my computer screen.

- I write out the most important priorities for me to accomplish that day for each of my teams.

- In our larger organizations, Kenyon & I focus on mentoring the top 3 leaders in each of those groups. This includes studying their numbers, sitting down together (in person or via video conference) once per month, as well as being available for questions as often as needed.

- In our smaller teams, I ask myself two questions every morning (before checking my email or my social media accounts 1. Where am I digging? (Who are the newest, most excited partners at the deepest points in each of my teams). 2. Who am I developing? (I use system indicators to determine who is getting results & deserves my time during the day.

- I listen to an average of three to four personal development audios per day that keep me Fired-Up & focused! For the past 15 years, I've spent an average of three to four hours per day on personal development education. I love listening to audio recordings and a huge part of my day is making sure that I fit in the time to listen to at least three 45 min to 1 hr audios per day. I listen to audios in my car constantly & when I'm out of my car I have my Bluetooth headphones in constantly.

- I do most of my reading time before I go to bed. I normally spend between 20 minutes and 2 hours studying books on all aspects of success personal development as well as my scriptures.

BONUS INTERVIEW FOR *MIRACLE MORNING FOR NETWORK MARKETING* READERS

Each of the Top One Percent Networkers that are featured in this book were interviewed by Pat Petrini about not only their morning routines, but their tips, techniques and strategies that have been critical in helping them become the best of the best in network marketing.

For your free and exclusive interview with Rob, go to www. TMMforNetworkMarketers.com/Rob

— 8 —

NETWORK MARKETING MASTER SKILL #2:

PRESENTING THE PRODUCTS AND THE OPPORTUNITY

"Nobody who bought a drill actually wanted a drill. They wanted a hole. Therefore, if you want to sell drills, you should advertise information about making holes—NOT information about drills!"
—PERRY MARSHALL, Online Marketing Strategist, Entrepreneur, and Author

Congratulations! You've prospected your heart out and have someone who wants to see what you've got. Now I'm going to walk you through how to become a brilliant presenter of your products and your opportunity. If you are new to network marketing, you might think you are a loooong way from being a star presenter or even believing people will see the opportunity you see.

Before I dive into the mechanics of presenting and overcoming objections, let me share a quick story about *my* very first presentation. It was 2004, and I was just 22 years old. I was completely sold on the business and was beginning to build my team. It was only a few weeks into my network marketing career, and one of my new marketers was ready to connect me with someone they thought would join the business.

I was absolutely terrified to do this presentation, and it's not that I was scared of presenting—I mean, I already had sales experience and knew I could present well. The question in my mind was, *Why would they bring this prospect to me when there are far better and more experienced people? What about our upline, my mentor, who is far more qualified to talk about the opportunity?*

Of course, relying on mentors and uplines can't go on forever; at some point you have to take complete and total responsibility for your business and learn how to present the products and opportunity yourself and for your team. If you don't have a strong upline team and/or mentor, then finding a mentor is going to be your responsibility from day one. If you do, you might have a few weeks or months to lean heavily on them. Eventually, you will become one of the go-to resources for your team, and it is necessary for you to teach them to also be self-sustaining as quickly as possible. You follow, then you lead, and then you teach others to lead. That is the essence of how network marketing works!

The Art of Presenting

Back to my first presentation: I did a three-way call with a guy named Mike from a small town in Idaho. At that time, my company was using a CD created by the number one earner as our main presentation resource. This CD provided an overview of the whole company, the products, and opportunity. I had listened to this CD so many times and taken detailed notes so that I almost had it memorized and could go through the presentation practically word for word, which is exactly what I did with Mike.

To my dismay, Mike did not sign up. I was petrified my team member who scheduled my call with Mike would see that as my fault in some way and wish they had referred Mike to someone with more experience. But that wasn't at all what happened. My team member was actually very impressed with my preparation for the call. Sure, team member would have loved for Mike to sign up, but they were so excited to see me do my first presentation. It actually empowered them to feel confident about beginning to do their own presentations.

Remember, as we've discussed, advantages and disadvantages are in your head. They aren't real. While you are worrying that you are screwing up the presentation, the person listening might be attracted by the sheer fact that you *aren't* a polished presenter and that (apparently) anybody can do this. It's all good!

In the beginning, the key to giving a masterful presentation is not to do the presentation yourself. The first few presentations should be performed by another experienced team member, or by using a tool, such as a video, webinar, or conference call. For example, you could bring a prospect to a coffee appointment, a home party, or even a hotel meeting where one of your team members is presenting.

My point is, when you're first getting started, you are not supposed to be the presenter. At the beginning, there is a learning curve, and you are at the bottom of it. You are actually the *connector*. Your job is to connect your prospect with a skilled presenter. Your role as budding genius presenter is to take meticulous notes on this fantastic presentation so eventually you can become a fantastic presenter too. The process of learning to present won't take long, I promise you. You can learn all of the necessary information to answer questions and overcome objections (a topic I'm going to tackle very soon) in a relatively short period of time to become, at first, an effective presenter and, eventually, a true rock star. The shortcut to becoming a great presenter is to study and mimic the great presenters in your business. Go and watch them present as many times as you can, listen in on their conference calls and any audio or video recordings they might have. Be sure to always have a notebook or journal to jot down key phrases and interesting tidbits that will be helpful to you. You can take bits and pieces from the great presentations you hear so you can (over time) craft an incredible presentation of your own.

I recorded as many presentations as I could. Then I studied the different aspects of the presentation and noted how I could use what they were doing in my own presentations. Today, all phones have a voice recorder built right into them. Record three-way phone calls, webinars, and even convention speakers, and then listen or watch them again and again. Analyze each presentation and learn a bit of the sales psychology in them (ask the presenter, if you need to, for any insights). The great news is that these recordings will be available to you forever, and you can access and review them as many times as you like. When it eventually became time for me to do presentations for my team, I had an arsenal of great presentations to draw from to create my own. On top of the reduced learning curve, there is another really powerful benefit to using a tool or your upline for your presentations when you are getting started. Let's say you've got a great prospect that is genuinely interested in starting a new business, but they are concerned about their own ability to present your products and opportunity. By connecting them to a tool or an experienced team member, you are showing them that they can do the same thing when they are getting started. It makes your business more easily duplicable, and duplication is the lubrication of the network marketing engine that you are fueling.

Visualize Presentation Success

By now I hope doing the Life S.A.V.E.R.S. is one of your daily practices. It is important for you to know how incredibly powerful visualization is, especially when you're doing something new—like building a network marketing business, for example.

Remember that visualization becomes far more powerful with specificity. Don't just picture yourself presenting. What are you saying exactly? How are you saying it? What is your posture like? Your hand gestures? What questions is the prospect asking, and how are you addressing them?

When you visualize the actual presentation, including how you want it to end, it's like an extra practice session for you. Every morning, visualize at least one of the presentations on your calendar for that day. Picture the person you're meeting getting excited about what you have to offer, asking great questions, and becoming a positive member of your team.

Third Party Validation

Have you heard the term "You're never a profit in your own land?" Can you relate to the frustration of feeling as though you have something amazing to share, you want most to share it with your friends and family, but they (the ones who are closest to you) are the ones who never listen to you? Conversely, do you feel like the people who don't know you very well are the ones who do listen to you? One day, it dawned on me that I was pigeon-holing my dad in this very way.

Throughout my life, my dad has always had a very eclectic taste in music and has been a constant learner. He listens to audio books and courses and reads great books. So many times throughout my life my dad has recommended a song, artist, book, or course. And for some reason when my dad used to recommend something to me, I would always write it off immediately as something I probably was not interested in. It was just my knee-jerk reaction.

Yet when I did go back and listen to an artist or read a book he recommended, it was almost always excellent. (Note to Dad: almost always. Smile.) Why is it that my natural tendency was to discount his recommendation? I have no idea. It just seems to be human nature. (Sorry Dad!) There's something about being too close to your family members and friends that causes us to reject their suggestions. While I've learned to listen to my dad a bit more, it took awhile for me to recognize that I was falling into this trap. Point being, the people closest to you will likely be open to hearing your pitch as a favor to you, but your words will probably not carry as much weight with them because they are your words. Third-party validation, via your upline, mentor or even a tool of some kind, is the bridge you need to get those closest to you on board.

Remember, as you let someone or something else do the presenting, it's not so much about the words or the content as much as it's about how they are receiving information and the source of information. Using third-party validation is your key to success in any situation where your words don't have the weight or credibility you need quite yet.

Be Ready With a Story

Stories connect people. We hear ourselves represented in the stories of other people, and leaders will often refer to network marketing as a "storyteller's business." There is an age-old saying in sales and network marketing that says, "Facts tell and stories sell." Because people are emotional creatures, we tend to buy based on emotion and then rationalize our buying decisions with logic. Our internal monologue usually starts with "I want this" and *then* goes to the reasons to buy it (even for the most rational, analytical and seemingly less emotional people!).

Let's take a second to discuss *why* stories can influence us so powerfully. Remember when we were discussing mirror neurons in the Life S.A.V.E.R.S. section under visualization? Mirror neurons are credited with giving us the ability to watch or visualize something happening and actually learn from it or empathize as though we are experiencing it ourselves. So, by telling a compelling story, your prospect can actually, on some level, experience your story as though they are the subject of it and living through it. The more specific and immersive your story, the more strongly the listener will experience it.

Can you see the power of that? Your prospect can *experience* your product through the stories you tell of others who have experienced it. Your prospect can *feel* what it is like to be financially independent if you can effectively tell the story of somebody who has become financially independent from your opportunity. That's why the best salespeople, presenters, and network marketers, are not databases of facts, but masterful storytellers.

Stories are very powerful in making your presentations come alive. Come to the table with a quiver of different stories related to your products or service, and be sure those stories include the amazing results that people have gotten from them and the way that people's lives are better now because of your product or service. Incorporate business building success stories that tell how the company and this business has radically and dramatically changed people's lives for the better—from an income, lifestyle, relationship, or some other standpoint.

If you'd like some great examples of professional storytellers telling their own stories of how network marketing has changed their lives, be sure to check out the Top One Percent Networker Interviews from the network marketing pros who have contributed to this book. You can find them at www.TMMforNetworkMarketers.com/interviews.

Listen to how people tell their own story, and it will give you a powerful example of how you should learn to tell other people's stories. Of course, you're probably going to want to collect stories from people within your own company that involve the products and services that you represent, but my point here is to provide you with professional examples of how a story should be told (along with a TON of other great applicable training).

The idea is to have stories, *real stories of real network marketers you know or know of,* that relate to the life situations of the various prospects you will encounter. You want your stories to be about people who have dealt with the same situations your prospects are dealing with currently. The longer you're in the business, the more stories you'll have, and you'll find them helpful to overcome objections and create desire for your product, service, or opportunity.

Handling Objections with Connections

Since we're talking about gathering your quiver of stories, I want to point out how powerful your quiver will be when it comes to handling objections. (I'm going to talk more about objections later when I discuss following up.)

I once met a guy named Mark, who was dead broke and desperately wanted to start his network marketing business, but didn't have the money to get started. Unlike many, he was willing to do whatever it took, so he held a garage sale and sold his television to pay his startup costs. Then he went to work, built a massive organization, and now, he's one of the most financially successful people in network marketing. Network marketing changed his life. Guess what I do when people tell me that they don't have enough money to get started? I tell them Mark's story and say "Let's have a garage sale!"

Some people talk about how little time they have to build a business. I'd suggest having multiple stories ready to go about people who have found ways to make time or people who have found ways to be successful with little time.

Some people talk about how they can't afford your product or service. I'd suggest that you have multiple stories about how people have saved money by using your product or service.

Some people have concerns about network marketing because of things they've heard or their own past experience. Be prepared to share stories about people who had similar reservations and learn how to convey exactly what caused them to come around in the end.

The quiver of stories that you're able to share relate to all kinds of people in all sorts of different situations. These stories will enable you to overcome the common objections that you're inevitably going to run into when building your business.

What's Your Story?

One of the most powerful stories you're going to share is actually your own. The first thing you want to do is make darn sure you're doing everything you can to make it a great one! Now, you may be just getting started with your network marketing business, or you may have been in for a long time; it doesn't matter. According to Jim Rohn, "The last six months have nothing to do with the next six months."

Your past is not an accurate predictor of your future. I suggest that you decide to make today the beginning of your new amazing story. The next week, next month, and next year you could be writing your new story. What's important is that you have that powerful story when you're sitting down and sharing it. You might even say, "You know what, I was sitting on my butt and not really being proactive. And then I read this book, and I decided to change my life and build this business. I really turned it on, and now it's been two months. Look at what has already happened; this is the success I have already had, this is where I'm going, and I want you with me!"

We all get one chance, as far as we know, to write our life's story. Make today the day that you proactively and consciously decided to write the story you are proud of!

The Post-Presentation Review

It doesn't matter if the presentation went well or not, or even who gave the presentation. A post-presentation review is an incredible opportunity to learn from every presentation.

Within a few hours, at most 24 hours, take some time (even five minutes) to jot down some notes in your journal about what went right, what you would do differently, what was effective, and what you want to change for the next opportunity.

The more presentations you do and observe, the better you will get. Let's face it, the first time you give a presentation, you're nervous and concerned you'll forget key pieces and points. Don't worry, that is completely normal. Once you've said something a dozen times, you'll start to feel like it's second nature, and once you've given a presentation more than a hundred times, you could give the presentation in your sleep! Every presentation you give builds your presentation-giving muscle. Eventually, it'll be you in the front the room with all of the newbies in their chairs saying to themselves, "I could *never* do that!"

Taking Your Presentations To The Next Level

In my opinion, there is one single quality that separates the most persuasive people on the planet from everybody else. You see, every word—whether written or spoken—has two meanings: the meaning intended by the person that said it and the meaning interpreted by the person who heard (or read) it.

What separates the real masters of persuasion from the average person is their ability to know precisely how their words will be interpreted by the person hearing them and craft them in a way that is likely to create the desired outcome.

As you give your presentation and interact with your prospects, pay close attention to the words you use. Did they land in the way you wanted them to? Did they paint the picture you were hoping to paint?

Record yourself and go back and listen. What sentences should you change? What single words should you substitute? Does your tone convey confidence?

Present. Review. Tweak. Present. Review. Tweak. If you craft your words with the attention to detail they deserve, I think you'll be amazed at the results that you generate over time.

I remember when I first started to see the results of this process. I was a 19-year-old kid selling Cutco Cutlery through in-home presentations. In between presentations, I would listen in my car to CDs of the best reps in the company doing their presentations. I'd listen to them over and over until I could not only recite them word for word, but I could mimic their tonality and timing. As I started working their presentations into my own, I began to see the impact their words had on my prospects, and I began to understand the psychology of it all. I started to understand *why* they said what they said in the way they said it and in the order they said it in.

Honestly, it was spooky. As my skills improved, it honestly felt like some sort of Jedi mind trick. It gave me an appreciation for how powerful words can be when you take the time to choose and craft them carefully.

Now, I'm not talking about manipulation. Though, this same skill can certainly be used for manipulation. I'm talking about the ability to communicate your thoughts and emotions as authentically as possible to another person so that they can most closely experience the thoughts and emotions that you have. Sure, you love your product, but your ability to effectively convey how you feel about your product to your customer is very dependent on the words, tone, pacing, body language, etc., that you use in that communication.

Like any other skill, it takes a lot of time and attention to detail to master, but I can promise you that it is worth the time, and it will carry over into many other areas of your life outside of sales and network marketing.

Once you've mastered the art of the presentation and you've started presenting on a daily basis, you will be well on your way to building a huge organization that will pay you, potentially, for the rest of your life. If you're ready for it, check out this success story and then proceed to the next chapter. Still more awaits you ...

TOP ONE PERCENT NETWORKER INTERVIEW

Ana Gabriel Mann

Facebook.com/anagabrielmann

Ana has an MA in clinical psychology and education and has spent her entire career teaching and mentoring.

She is a devoted mother and is married to the *New York Times* bestselling author John David Mann.

Ana believes deeply in relationships, giving and mentoring as key aspects of a happy life. A dedicated teacher globally, she believes that education is power, and that curiosity is the cornerstone to finding your true path.

Ana's Miracle Morning & Daily Rituals:

- First off, I spend 20-30 minutes at night right before bed making a gratitude acknowledgement of things I am grateful for from my life and from the immediate day. This is the bookend to a morning ritual --take a few minutes to meditate on *good things* before sleeping.

- 6:00 a.m. - Wake Up

- My Miracle Morning includes no less than 30-50 mins of exercise at the end, so I typically spend 90-120 minutes per morning on self development and time in personal creation.

- I get up early and have tea first to get alert and ready.

- I meditate for 40 minutes and my meditation includes an extensive visualization. Meditation/Prayer is for me the key to staying connected to a Higher Source. It is the baseline of focus and grounding and it allows me to "listen" and hear the truth. Visualization is also a key element in seeing your future in the best way possible. Imagine and visualize your new future and it will be yours. Watch for the signs that will inevitably show up.

God/the Divine likes to interact with us but most people don't listen or watch for the signs that your connection to a Higher Source is alive in the moment.

- I read my affirmations and gratitude. Affirmations are the truth as you spell it. In other words, what do you want to create? Write it, speak it and affirm it. Words have power. They are your vision for the future-- craft it with care and be certain it feels authentic to you. Belief is everything.

- I find that limiting beliefs are usually based in low self-esteem, fear/lack of trust for all of us. The question that always emerges if discussed is "do I deserve this future I imagine?" I like to take a minute or two to be fully thankful for my prayers being heard and answered. Low self-esteem drives us to feel insignificant and invisible, but it is not the truth. Gratitude and faith are key- our prayers are *always* heard and answered.

- Music is a big deal for me. It sets up my day and my attitude. I always play a few of my favorite songs that just open up my energy and my heart to the day before me. Sometimes I turn up the volume in the kitchen while I make another cup of tea or I begin the last portion of stretching and moving.

- I spend 5 minutes stretching and getting every cell fully awake and either walk in the morning air or head to the gym. Exercise is one of the everyday actions that keeps you and your brain and attitude sharp. We know from research and science that the brain is profoundly affected positively by exercise-- it's a must do.

- I end with reading some sort of inspirational personal growth. Leaders are readers is the old phrase--- but it is true. This can be personal growth related to your work, or an inspirational book that sets the tone for your actions or attitude. I believe that no matter what your career or endeavor, growing yourself is the first step. Reading and investing in personal growth is the most important daily action.

BONUS INTERVIEW FOR *MIRACLE MORNING FOR NETWORK MARKETING* READERS

Each of the Top One Percent Networkers that are featured in this book were interviewed by Pat Petrini about not only their morning routines, but their tips, techniques and strategies that have been critical in helping them become the best of the best in network marketing.

For your free and exclusive interview with Ana, go to www. TMMforNetworkMarketers.com/Ana

NETWORK MARKETING MASTER SKILL #3:

THE FORTUNE IS IN THE FOLLOW-UP

"It is rarely a mysterious technique that drives us to the top, but rather a profound mastery of what may well be a basic skill set. Depth beats breadth any day of the week, because it opens a channel for the intangible, unconscious, creative components of our hidden potential."
–JOSH WAITZKIN, Chess Prodigy, Martial Arts Champion, and Author

The phrase "the fortune is in the follow-up" is another one of those phrases that has become a cliché because it is true. You see, even the newest and most inexperienced of the bunch are pretty good at prospecting, presenting, or connecting their prospects to a great presentation; but where they drop the ball is in the follow-up.

One of the main reasons they drop the ball is because they are absolutely terrified their prospect will tell them no. It's that fear of rejection that keeps marketers from following up, even though statistics show that most people don't say yes until the seventh follow-up!

You honestly don't know what your prospect is going to say, and to find out you *do* have to ask. Some marketers think, "Well, if they were interested, they would have called me." Instead of making sure they are a no, it's easier to let that lead go than to get a firm answer.

Two things: First, to be really successful in network marketing, you must become excellent at following up with each and every prospect until you get a yes or a no. Second, the only way to become excellent is to suck it up and make those phone calls!

I know from experience that the fortune in network marketing is in the follow-up. The vast majority of the customers and marketers that have become part of my organization over the years did *not* jump in immediately after looking at it the first time. In most cases, it took several rounds of following up, answering questions, giving them more information, and then following up again to get to yes. In some cases, it was months or even years of pleasant persistence, which we will discuss soon, before they decided to join or purchase.

How do you know how long it will take for somebody to make a decision? You don't. So you follow up with everybody, consistently, and let them become a yes or a no on their own time.

I want you to master this piece of the puzzle, so you can build the organization of your dreams; have customers who use, love, share, and consistently purchase your products; and exceed each and every goal you set for yourself. I'm going to start with the *how*, and then share some tips on the *when*. Get a firm grasp on follow-up, and you will be able to succeed beyond your wildest dreams!

Use the Life S.A.V.E.R.S. to Accelerate Your Success

During your Life S.A.V.E.R.S. visualization, include the follow-up. Specifically, visualize some of the important calls you're going to make that day. Picture people picking up the phone and asking lots of questions, as well as your responses to them. What are they asking? What are you saying? *How* do you sound? What is the next step that you both discuss at the end of the call? Visualize checking your group volume. What is it at the beginning of the day, what is it at the end of the day, and how exactly did it get there?

The How's of Follow-Up

Here are some important things to keep in mind about the follow-up process:

Pleasant Persistence

Pleasant persistence is a term that I learned early in my sales career. Pleasant persistence is persistence with a smile. With each contact, be fun and casual. Prospects don't want a hard sell or a hard time. They don't want to interact with an intense "are you in or out?" type of a person. The most effective follow-up includes contacting people and saying, "Hey, it's me. I'm just checking in on you. I would love to continue our conversation about XYZ when you can spare a minute."

Become someone who does their job with the consistency of a pro, but the confidence and playfulness of somebody that loves and believes in what they do. You're touching base, making sure they are okay and that they know if they have any questions, you have the answers. Your authenticity and approachable manner will allow your prospects to feel you are easy to work with, because you are just reconnecting with them and there's no pressure one way or the other. Even if they know that they are going to be telling you no one more time, they answer your calls and enjoy talking to you because they know you genuinely enjoy talking to them as well.

As a side note, professional businesspeople have tremendous respect for quality follow-up. As you diligently follow up with them, in a friendly and light manner, you will gain their respect and, over time, their friendship. Even if they don't end up buying or joining, you're absolutely going to build your relationship with them. Keep in mind: you never know what your efforts will lead to down the road. In fact, the relationships that you will build in the process if you do it right are one of the massively underestimated benefits of network marketing.

Here are some ways to execute easy, no-pressure follow-up:

- "As promised, I wanted to check in and see if you've had a chance to check out the (video, recording, book, presentation, etc.) that I left with you."

- "Hey, you can absolutely be straight with me. What are your honest thoughts on this?"

- "I want you to know that it's not important to me if you buy or join; it's just important to me that you check it out. Is that cool?"

- "Based on what you've seen so far, what are the things you like and what are some of the questions or concerns you have?" This is one of my favorite questions to ask people, because that's exactly what I'm trying to find out when I'm following up with people: are they close? Not yet? Wherever they are is completely fine with me. And I *want* to understand their objections so that I know what additional info they might need. "Remember, I just want to make sure you've got all the info you need. I want you to make whatever decision is right for you."

- "I just want you to know that the only reason I'm being so persistent with you is because of how much respect I have for you and how good I think you would be at it. Don't worry though, I'm good with whatever you decide!"

The fact is I'm 100 percent fine with a no if they are not interested. I'm actually excited to check them off my list so I can move on to the next person.

My job—your job—is to follow-up. But here's something cool to keep in the back of your mind …

Yes or No Not Now?

Your objective, of course, is to get your prospect to a yes or a no. Your desired outcome, as we both know, is to enroll people onto your team and sign up new customers who purchase your products or services.

We also both know what a yes means ... but how about no? I believe a no can be easily translated as not now. They aren't interested in the business *right now*. They don't have an interest in purchasing any products *right now*. Timing is everything, and *right now* is not their timing. But because you're in it for the long haul, you're still probably going to follow up with them. Why? Because you like them. You would really like to have them as marketers on your team or customers who use and love your products or services. Right?

So, I advise you to send them a card on their birthday. Give 'em a call, touch base, and see how they are doing. What, it's the holidays? Great! Call and wish them a Happy New Year! Saw they went on an African Safari on Facebook? Call and ask to see the pictures! During one of these conversations, they might ask how you're doing, and you'll say, "Still doing the same thing. In fact, everything in my world is right except for the fact that we aren't working together!" Now, it might be the perfect time to broach the subject again, or you may just decide to leave it alone. That's really something you can only learn through a *lot* of experience following up with people.

You can also get their permission to share new products that are released. "Jim, I totally get that now isn't the best time for you, but would it be okay if I kept you updated on any new announcements that I think you might care about?" You'll almost always get a yes to that. As a new study about one of your current products comes out, you can send a quick email to let them know. Anytime there is a new and exciting something that happens, share it with them. All of these are fantastic reasons to potentially get in touch with the prospects for whom the timing has not yet been perfect. Show them how that new announcement is pertinent to them and how it might impact them.

Now, even though you should interpret no to mean not yet, that doesn't mean that I'm encouraging you to constantly pester or annoy people. Find creative ways to build and maintain your relationship. Talk about things outside of your business. Take a sincere interest in making their lives better whether or not they ever show interest in what you have to offer.

One of my favorite things to do is to buy small gifts for people if that particular gift specifically reminds me of the person. Most often for me, it is a book I read that I'm sure they would love. I can't tell you how grateful people are to randomly receive a gift that clearly shows you were thinking of them specifically. In one case, I met a prospect of one of my team members at a meeting where I was presenting. From our conversation, I was sure this woman would love a certain book I had recently read on nutrition. So, I sent it to her. She never ended up joining our business, and I never followed up with her because she really wasn't my prospect. However, years later, I got a note out of the blue from her telling me how much that book had changed her life and set her on a new path with her health. How freaking cool is that?

Here's my point. I haven't spoken to her in years, but if I reached out to her for some reason tomorrow and asked her to take a look at something, I bet there is a 99% chance that she would do it because I took the time to add value to her life without the expectation of anything in return. That's what quality follow-up looks like.

The First of Many Touches

It is important to have a follow-up system in place, which means you will always have a next step. You will always finish one step with the next step, and you'll want to have pre-determined what that next step will be. For example, if a prospect views their first presentation via a webinar, you will want to contact them after they've finished to discuss any of their questions and determine their next step. Before they view the webinar, you will want to schedule that follow-up call. When you find out their next steps on the follow-up call, you'll want to schedule a time for whatever they need next. Make sense?

As you navigate their questions and inquiries about the product or service, compensation plan, or who they can talk to about their experience with the company, you will want to have a solid system in place for staying in touch with them. You want them to make a decision about their best role in your business. The idea is, "next step, next step, next step ..." until you get either a yes or a no (which, as we know, is a not now).

Also, as soon as you've finished a meeting or completed a phone call, take action on that next step. I recommend confirming or reminding them via an email what you're doing. Try something like this:

Dear Phil,

As you requested, attached is our compensation plan. I'm looking forward to talking with you on Thursday at 2 pm. at Starbucks. See you there!

Joanne

Typically, follow-up meetings and conversations have a regular rhythm. As your prospects review the material you've provided or attend the call or meeting, they are going to have additional questions. They might be a yes on your product or service as a customer, maybe they join your marketing team ... or maybe they will say no to all of the above. Your objective is to follow up until you have their right now answer.

Organized Follow-Up Works Like a Charm

The best thing you can do, right from the top, is to have a follow-up system in place so that no prospect falls through the cracks. The worst thing you can hear is, "I was interested, but nobody followed up with me so I joined with somebody else." (Ouch!) To that end, you have a bunch of options for good customer relationship management (CRM) tools. Certainly some of them are very powerful and helpful, but some are expensive.

I believe all you really need is a simple spreadsheet. You can use Microsoft Excel or Google Docs. Google Docs is what I've used for years. I have one simple spreadsheet with three different tabs.

The first tab, or sheet, is my master list, and everybody I can think of goes on that master list. I include anyone and everyone who might in any way be a prospect for my product or service or for my marketing team, either now or down the road

The second tab is my active list. These are the people that I'm working on right now; the people who are in the process of actively evaluating my products and/or opportunity.

The third tab is my drip list. My drip list consists of the people who initially gave me a no. These are the people who were on my active list and I took them through my follow-up system, but, for one reason or another, the timing wasn't right, and they did not become a customer or marketer. I put the majority of them on my drip list, which means that on certain occasions (such as when there is an important announcement or it's their birthday or another special occasion), I'm going to reach out to them.

During many of these touches, there may not be any mention of products or businesses or anything like that. I will reach out to say hello, wish them Merry Christmas or Happy Mother's Day, or even to mention that I was thinking of them. The goal is to build the relationship, slowly and over time, until they come around and start to ask questions again. If, at any point, the discussion goes back to my products, services, or opportunity, then I'll move them back to my active list and begin to share the information that I think would be best for them until they, once again, turn into a yes or a not now.

The Master List Sheet

You might be wondering what my sheets look like. You can download an example sheet at www.TMMforNetworkMarketers.com/FollowUp . Each line of the master sheet contains columns like name, phone number, email address, notes (such as spouse's and kid's names, how you met them, and any other pertinent information you want to remember), and follow-up date (which is the next date I want to reach out to them).

For example, let's say I contacted someone today. They wanted to learn some more about the compensation plan, and I send them a compensation plan video to review. When we agree to talk in two days, I will enter that follow-up date in the spreadsheet. Each day,

I sort my spreadsheet according to the follow-up date, and all the people I need to follow-up with are going to pop up right there at the top.

You can do the same. Every day sort your spreadsheet by date and you can see who you need to follow up with that day. *Then, just make your phone calls.* As long as you make that part of your daily ritual, everyone is going to get a follow-up call, and right on time. You are going to be a follow-up superstar because no one will ever slip through the cracks, and you will look like the network marketing pro you are! Because you do a few of those phone calls every day, you will be moving the needle on your business every day. Eventually, your list will grow, and your business will grow.

A Word On Objections

In writing this book, I began to write an entire section on objections—including the most common objections that we hear in network marketing as well as some common responses to them. Here's the thing though, if you don't understand the psychology behind objections, then a few boilerplate answers are not going to help you. In fact, they might hurt you because a canned response can take away from your authenticity.

The topic of handling objections is a big one and it deserves your attention. Some of the books I recommended earlier related to sales and network marketing are excellent sources of more information on the sales process, presentation, communication, and the art of the close, which includes handling objections.

Here's the beauty of network marketing … When you are getting started, you honestly don't need to be that good at handling objections, you just need to be able to connect your prospects to people who are. It's the same concept we previously discussed with regards to becoming a great presenter by leveraging other great presenters and their presentations.

When I got started, I put people in front of my mentor, and I studied his presentation. Then, I'd ask my mentor what the next step was with the prospect. He would tell me, and I would do it. Often times it was to give them some information and set up a follow-up appointment to discuss questions. So, I would set the follow-up appointment where I would study, record, and take notes on how he answered their questions and handled their objections. Then I would ask him what the next step was, and then I would do that, and on and on and on until I got pretty good at it myself.

Network marketing is so powerful in that way because it gives you the opportunity to learn through provided education, experience, and mentorship what would otherwise be *much* harder (and more expensive) to learn on your own.

Real Objections And Bogus Objections

Having said all of that, here are a few simple concepts that I hope will help as you begin to study the art of handling objections.

First, it is important to understand that most objections are completely bogus. It's not that your prospects are lying to you. In most cases, they honestly don't consciously know what their real objection is; they are telling you one thing but the truth is something entirely different.

For example, your prospect tells you, "I don't have the time to start a new business."

This may sound like an honest objection, but let me ask you this. If you told that same prospect that you would pay them $500 for every magazine that they could read for the next 30 days, how much time do you think they would find to read magazines? Probably as many hours as they could keep their eyes open, right? So, is the *real* objection that they don't have any time? No, the real objection is that you have not *shown them the value* in why they should find the time. Maybe they don't understand how the compensation plan works. Maybe they don't understand how they would go about getting customers, building their team, and making an amount of money that would justify finding the time. Maybe their objection is something entirely different, and they are giving you a polite brush off.

In the end, there are only two real objections: either they legitimately do not have a need or a want for your product, service or opportunity, or you simply haven't done a good job in creating a need or a want through the information you have connected them to. In a way, these are two sides of the same coin.

The point is, their objection is likely *not* that they don't have time to start a new business.

So how do you break through these bogus objections? By asking questions, and often lots of them. Try something like this:

"I totally understand, Jenny. I know you're busy, and your time is really valuable to you. Just out of curiosity, if somebody were able to show you how you could consistently earn more per hour doing this than what you currently do at your job, is that something you could justify spending time on, or would it still not make sense to you?"

Maybe Jenny says, "Sure, if you could show me how I could consistently earn more, then that might make sense." Or, maybe Jenny says, "Honestly, there are 100 ways for me to make more than what I'm doing, but I truly love what I do and don't want to deviate from it."

You can see how those two responses should be responded to entirely differently. The first answer tells you that you need to understand how much she makes per hour and put a clear, realistic game plan together so she knows how she could earn more working with you. The second answer takes you closer to a more authentic objection. She may not have a need for what you have to offer. However, she may know someone who does, so keep asking questions.

If you become skilled at responding to objections with questions, then the objections become your roadmap. They tell you exactly what information your prospect needs to make a decision.

Objection. Question. Objection. Question. Objection. Question. Keep at it until you discover the need or until you are satisfied that your prospect just isn't the right fit for what you have to offer at this point in time (but be sure to keep in touch!).

Try a little practice session in your head. What are some of the other objections you might hear? What are some questions that you could ask in response? What might their counter questions be, and how should you respond? The more that you practice, both mentally and in person, the better you'll get.

You've now learned three of the critical skills to becoming a network marketer, but I still haven't covered the key ingredient that unlocks the exponential potential of network marketing; teaching people to do what you've learned to do. So, if you're ready, go ahead and turn to the final Master Skill Chapter: Fast Start Success.

TOP ONE PERCENT NETWORKER INTERVIEW

Lisa Cox

Facebook.com/1coxskincare

Instagram: @CoxSkinCare

Upon joining the company that Lisa represents, she quickly replaced a 13 year income from another network marketing company, earned a free Lexus and a $50,000 bonus.

In the last 3 1/2 years, she has grown as a leader, became a student of the industry, built a team to over 15,000 strong and is generating millions of dollars per month in product sales. She has personally mentored 29 people to a six-figure income and has helped hundreds of people earn their own free Lexus.

She recently became one of only 13 people in her company to earn the rank of Five Star National Marketing Director, an achievement that comes with a $375,000.00 bonus.

She is a Golden Key Earner with David Byrd and her greatest accomplishment is a happy marriage to Steve Cox for 26 years along with her two daughters, Megan and Amanda. They are her "why".

Lisa's Miracle Morning & Daily Rituals:

- My Miracle Morning starts at 6:30. I keep a bottle of water by my bed and drink as soon as I wake up. I do not hit snooze.

- Then, I move to a quiet spot. We are empty nesters so I have lots of quiet spots but when I am at home and not traveling I go to my office.

- I sit in my chair and I pray. I have prayed in the morning for many years but usually as I moved around the kitchen or house instead of sitting quietly. I love the new focus on my prayers.

- Next, I meditate. I have been a yoga girl and when I meditate I breathe in love and breathe out hate, breathe in kindness and breathe out meanness, breathe in quiet and breathe out noise....or some version of this.

- I then say my affirmations. I say them like I have already achieved them. Then I grab my journal and write my affirmations and my gratitudes. I usually have a page of gratitudes.

- I'll then journal about the way I feel.

- Next, I usually have coffee and then I put in my earbuds and power walk for an hour. I live in Missouri and it's very hilly so I like to push it!

- I'm usually spending 3-5 minutes on each activity, though, I am enjoying adding time to each as my morning routine grows. I finish my Miracle Morning feeling ready for the world, ready for a challenge and ready to be better in all areas! I love it!

BONUS INTERVIEW FOR *MIRACLE MORNING FOR NETWORK MARKETING* READERS

Each of the Top One Percent Networkers that are featured in this book were interviewed by Pat Petrini about not only their morning routines, but their tips, techniques and strategies that have been critical in helping them become the best of the best in network marketing.

For your free and exclusive interview with Lisa, go to www. TMMforNetworkMarketers.com/Lisa

Network Marketing Master Skill #4:

FAST START SUCCESS

*Tell me and I'll forget; show me and I may
remember; involve me and I'll understand.*
—CHINESE PROVERB

The final skill you must master is the skill of getting people started in their new network marketing business. Getting each person off to a quick and successful start is crucial to each new marketer's short- and long-term success. In fact, a new marketer on your team must achieve a measurable level of success within their first 30 days. Otherwise, there is a high likelihood they will quit. Those are just the facts. That is how quickly people lose their drive and excitement. Your goal should be to help every single person you recruit to make money, sponsor new customers and marketers onto their team, and feel like their time and money is well spent, within their first 30 days of signing up. You need to find out what they want, and show them how to get it—the quicker the better.

What are you going to show them in terms of getting started? This varies from company to company. You'll want to consult with your upline, as well as look at what kind of the system your company has in place. The actual getting started process might be three, five, ten, or even a hundred steps. The important thing is that it is a process that has been proven to work, one that other people are currently using to achieve measurable and duplicable results. Hopefully the best process to use with your new people is the one you used when you got started. The most important thing to remember is that you want people to join your team with a high level of enthusiasm and excitement, and be able to maintain and increase their excitement because of the results they are getting right out of the gate.

Regardless of what your exact getting started process looks like, one of the key pieces of every onboarding process is to find out what your new marketer really wants out of their business. Finding out what their goals, dreams, and objectives are will help you to help them stay motivated, recommit when the going gets tough, and engage in the right activities. In other words, why are they joining your team? What do they want to get out of it? They might have a monetary or lifestyle goal; they might want to bring in enough money so their significant other can resign from a job they hate, or their desire might be to get themselves out of a job *they* hate! It might be as simple as earning a little bit of extra spending money to go on one extra vacation a year with their family. Your job is to find out what they want for two main reasons.

First, clarity on your part helps them to gain clarity on their part. The more clear they can get about what they want, the more likely they're going to be motivated to go after it. That's how goal setting works. The more precise their goals are, the more likely they are to succeed, particularly if you can help break the goals into smaller, bite-sized chunks.

Second, you must find out what they truly want because network marketing is a volunteer army. Your team is not going to do what you want them to do because of *your* goals. They are going to do what they want to do because of *their* goals. The only leverage you will ever have with anyone on your team is to know and understand what they want and why they chose to build a business. This knowledge will help you remind them of their desired outcomes. In addition, they need to know you are trying to help them to achieve those outcomes! You can't yell at them, nor can you force them to do anything, because they aren't employees. What you can do is take a sincere interest in them and what they are trying to achieve. When you do that, you have permission to hold them accountable, gently push them, and remind them of their "why." When your team can feel that your driving force is to help them hit their goals, you will have buy in, and buy in is the very best way to motivate your team members.

A fast start with a clear why will ensure you have a high level of retention, and enable you to build your downline, even as you help them build their downlines. Remember this: the more customers and team members each of your team members has, the stronger their business and the more likely they are to stay with it and keep building.

Bonus Tip: Would you like to know a secret to increasing the retention of your marketers, boosting their productivity and giving them a blueprint of all the skills they need to acquire in order to succeed? Here it is. Start them each off with a copy of this book! I know ... another shameless plug, right? The truth is, I wrote this book specifically for every new marketer that I ever recruit. This is the information that I want them to begin applying to their lives and their business as fast as possible. So I really mean it when I say that I believe this is a great tool for getting them started. Then again, I'm pretty biased.

How Do I Earn Money?

The next piece of a successful start is ensuring that each new marketer understands how they make money, and for this to happen, they must understand *exactly* how the compensation plan works. Sadly, it is common for an individual to get started in network marketing without clarity around how the compensation plan works, or even know how to make their first dollar. This is particularly unfortunate because the majority of people are driven by incentives, the most popular of which is cash. If they know exactly what it takes to make their first $100, $500, or $1,000, they become unstoppable. Nothing will get in the way of their taking the necessary actions. However, if the compensation plan isn't clear, or they are confused (keep in mind that most new people are new to this type of compensation), they won't take action or they will take confused action. A confused mind gets and stays stuck. It simply won't move. Without clarity initial success is impossible, and we're back to where we started: people who might otherwise have had a very successful network marketing career quit.

If a new marketer "kind of knows" how they get paid for the new customers and marketers they recruit, they won't be as inclined to take intentional action as when they have the right knowledge. Knowledge is power, and it is definitely powerful in network marketing. It isn't necessary for new marketers to understand every single piece of the compensation plan, but it *is* really important that they understand what their financial goals are for the first week, month, and first few months. It is also important that they know what needs to happen to accomplish those financial goals. If you can make it crystal clear to each of your team members how to make the money they want to make, you'll find they are way more likely to take the actions they need to take to accomplish those goals.

How the Law of Averages *Guarantees* Your Success

Ask the average person, "What are the odds of flipping a coin and getting heads ten times in a row?" Most people won't know the exact odds, but almost everyone would respond that it's very, very, very unlikely. Certainly no savvy bettor would take that bet, or even entertain a similar bet.

However, if I changed the terms and said that you can flip the coin as many times as you want until you get ten heads in a row, does that change the odds? Absolutely it does! Not only does it increase the odds, it guarantees the odds that you will get ten heads in a row. That is the magic of the law of averages, and actually, the magic of network marketing. On the scale of infinite flips, not only is there a possibility you will get those ten heads, there is an absolute guarantee you will.

The same principle applies to building your network marketing business. Everybody starts off with different skill sets. You may be a good presenter already, but you may not be. You may be good at prospecting already, or you might still be building those skills. You may be excellent at follow-up already, or you may not be quite yet. You may have had success in network marketing in the past, or maybe this is your first rodeo. All of these variables are going to have an impact on your results; your averages.

How many people do you need to prospect in order to find somebody who agrees to see a presentation? How many presentations need to happen before you find someone who decides to join? How many people need to decide to join before you find the person who grabs the baton of opportunity and runs with the business? How can you improve those averages? By getting skilled at helping people get started.

As you get better and become masterful at each of the network marketing master skills that we have discussed, the higher your averages are going to be and the better the numbers you will put on the board. Success is going to depend upon how good your skills are and whether you're talking to the right people. No matter where you start, you can absolutely get better. All of the fundamental skills I've shared with you in this book are fairly simple, and they are skills that anyone with some commitment and determination can learn and master.

The questions then becomes, what are you willing to do? How hard are you willing to work? Let me throw out some numbers.

How Many Will It Take?

If you talk to any top networker (I have talked to hundreds of them), and ask them a simple question, you will almost always get the same answer. Here's the question:

How many people have you personally recruited, and of those people, how many of them are responsible for building the majority of your organization and income?

The answers to the first part of this question will vary. Sometimes it will be as low as ten or twenty. Usually I find that it's in the realm of forty to one hundred, although on occasion it's several hundred. But here's the kicker, no matter how many people they've personally sponsored, of those it is almost always three to five key people they've sponsored who are responsible for the size and financial success of their organization.

Here's why that's key information for you: what you're really looking for are three to five key people to join your team and do what you do. Three to five key people who are going to run with the business, treat it like a business, and build an organization with the same level of commitment as you.

That's it! All you need are three to five key people!

Why do some people have to recruit hundreds to find those three to five key people while others recruit only dozens? Assuming that you have aligned yourself with a good company, then it comes down to the skills that we have already discussed. The better your skills are, the better your numbers will be.

I'm going to throw out some numbers as an example, to whet your appetite. Let's say that for every five people that you present to, product or business, one of them joins your organization as a marketer. And, let's say that for every ten people who join as a marketer, there is one that actually builds it (a key person). That's a total of 250 presentations to identify five key people that could lead to complete financial freedom!

So the question is, if those were your numbers, are you willing to do 250 presentations to be financially free? You need to present to 250 people to find your five. If it were guaranteed that you would be financially free after doing those 250 presentations, then how quickly would you do them? And, what the heck are you waiting for? You might be inclined to get off to a super fast start, and encourage your new marketers to do the same, by attempting to do as many of these 250 presentations as you possibly can in *your first 30 days*. Talk about fast-start success! At the very least, you'll catch the wave and ride the momentum for a long time to come.

You might not feel like doing all of the presentations in the first month, and if your new marketers are as time-limited as many of mine, then take it a bite at a time. Let's say you were going to introduce one prospect to a presentation per day, five days per week for fifty weeks per year. That would be 250 presentations in a single year. And, if you factor in the time that it takes to meet those people, set up and execute those presentations and follow up with everybody, you'd probably be looking at a total of a few hours of work per day. That's the equivalent of working a part-time job for one year that has the potential to give you financial freedom.

Of course, your numbers are going to vary. What if your numbers were twice as bad, and only one in ten people signed up instead of one in five? Then you'd have to do 500 presentations instead of 250, but wouldn't that *still* be worth it? It would be really valuable to track your numbers to see what your averages are so that you can not only measure them, but actually work to improve them. The numbers are going to vary based on how good your skills become and how qualified the prospects are that you are talking to. You can find my Activity Tracking Sheet here: www.TMMforNetworkMarketers.com/ActivityTracker.

I urge you to trust in the law of averages. Keep filling your calendar, prospecting, presenting, following up, and getting people started, and you will guarantee your success. You will eventually find your key people and by virtue of that, have a life, business, and income few people ever get to experience!

Millions of people have mastered these skills and created the life and business of their dreams. Personally, I don't believe that there is anything that millions of people can learn to do that you and I can't also learn to do. I hope you feel the same way. The only thing in your way now is application. Go for it.

Congratulations! You've learned the key components of network marketing that any person can master to achieve amazing success. Before you go, there's one more piece for you to add to your arsenal, *the Miracle Equation*. Are you ready? Turn the page …

— 10 —
THE MIRACLE EQUATION

*"For those who are willing to make an effort, great
miracles and wonderful treasures are in store."*
—ISAAC BASHEVIS Singer, Nobel Prize
Winner (1978)

You might say that Pat has saved the best for last. It's time to take everything you've learned so far and bring it together with the ultimate success equation that ALL top achievers— in every field—use to consistently produce extraordinary results.

You know now that you can wake up early, maintain extraordinary levels of energy, direct your focus, and master the not-so-obvious network marketing success skills. But I know you didn't read this far merely to take your success up a notch. You want to make quantum leaps and generate extraordinary results, right? Right. If you also apply what follows to your network marketing career, you're going to go much further: you're going to join the elite performers—*the top one percent.*

To make those leaps, there is one more crucial strategy that you must add to your network marketing toolbox, and it's called The Miracle Equation.

The Miracle Equation is the underlying strategy that I used to consistently break sales records, become one of the youngest individuals ever inducted into my company's hall of fame, and go on to become a number one bestselling author and international keynote speaker. But it's more than that. It is precisely the same equation that ALL top performers—that top one percent—have used to create awe-inspiring results, while the other 99 percent wonder how they do it.

The Miracle Equation was born during one of my Cutco push periods, a 14-day span during which the company fostered friendly competition and created incentives to bring in record sales, both for the salesperson and the office.

This particular push period was special for two reasons. First, I was trying to become the first sales representative in company history to take the number one spot for three consecutive push periods. Second, I'd have to do it while being able to work only 10 of the 14 days.

I knew I needed to dig deep to achieve such a feat and that fear and self-doubt were a much greater hurdle than usual. In fact, I considered lowering my sales goal based on the circumstances. Then I remembered what one of my mentors, Dan Casetta, had taught me: "The purpose of a goal isn't to hit the goal. The real purpose is to develop yourself into the type of person who can achieve your goals, regardless of whether you hit that particular one or not. It is who you become by giving it everything you have until the last moment—regardless of your results—that matters most."

I made a decision to stick with my original goal, even though the possibility of failing to achieve it was a real risk based on the limited time frame. With only ten days to set a record, I knew I needed to be especially focused, faithful, and intentional. It was an ambitious objective, no question, and as you'll see, one that required me to find out what I was really made of!

Two Decisions

As with any great challenge, I needed to make decisions related to achieving the goal. I reverse-engineered the Push Period by asking myself, "If I were to break the record in just ten days, what decisions would I have to make and commit to in advance?"

I identified the two that would make the biggest impact. Only later did I realize that these were *the same two decisions that all top-performers make at some point in their careers.*

Those two decisions became the basis for The Miracle Equation.

The First Decision: Unwavering Faith

Knowing that I was already facing fear and self-doubt, I realized that to achieve the seemingly impossible, I would have to decide to maintain unwavering faith each and every day, *regardless of my results.* I knew that there would be moments when I would doubt myself and times when I would be so far off track that the goal would no longer seem achievable. But it would be those moments when I would have to override self-doubt with unshakeable faith.

To keep that level of faith in those challenging moments, I repeated what I call my Miracle Mantra:

I will _____ (make the next sale, call 20 prospects, reach my goal), no matter what. There is no other option.

Understand that maintaining unwavering faith isn't *normal.* It's not what most people do. When it doesn't look like the desired result is likely, average performers give up the faith that it's possible. When the game is on the line, a team is down on the scorecards, and there are only seconds left, it is only the elite performers—the Michael Jordans of the world—who, without hesitation, tell their team, "Give me the ball."

The rest of the team breathes a sigh of relief because of their fear of missing the game-winning shot, while Michael Jordan made a decision at some point in his life that he would maintain unwavering faith, despite the fact that he might miss. (And although Michael Jordan missed 26 game-winning shots in his career, his faith that he would make every single one never wavered.)

That's the first decision that the world's elite make, and it's yours for the making, too.

When you're working toward a goal and you're not on track, what is the first thing that goes out the window? *The faith that the outcome you want so much is possible.* Your self-talk becomes *I'm not on track. It doesn't look like I'm going to reach my goal.* And with each passing moment, your faith decreases.

You don't have to settle for that. You have the ability and the choice to maintain that same unwavering faith, no matter what, and regardless of the results. You may sometimes doubt yourself or have a bad day, but you must find—and re-find—your faith that all things are possible and hold it throughout your journey, whether it is a 10-day push period or a 30-year career.

Elite athletes maintain unwavering faith that they can make every shot they take. That faith—and the faith you need to develop—isn't based on probability. It draws from a whole different place. Most salespeople operate based on what is known as the *law of averages*. But what we're talking about here is the *law of miracles*. When you miss shot after shot—in your case, sale after sale—you have to tell yourself what Michael Jordan tells himself, *I've missed three, but I want the ball next, and I'm going to make that next shot.*

And if you miss that one, *your faith doesn't waiver.* You repeat the Miracle Mantra to yourself:

I will _____ (sign up the next prospect, call 20 prospects, reach my goal), no matter what. There is no other option.

Then, you simply uphold your integrity and do what it is that you say you are going to do.

An elite athlete may be having the worst game ever, where it seems like in the first three-quarters of the game, they can't make a shot to save their life. Yet in the fourth quarter, right when the team needs them, they start making those shots. They always want the ball; they always have belief and faith in themselves. In the fourth quarter, they score three times as many shots as they've made in the first three-quarters of the game.

Why? They have conditioned themselves to have unwavering faith in their talents, skills, and abilities, regardless of what it says on the scoreboard or their stats sheet.

And …

They combine their unwavering faith with part two of The Miracle Equation: extraordinary effort.

The Second Decision: Extraordinary Effort

When you allow your faith to go out the window, effort almost always follows right behind it. *After all,* you tell yourself, *what's the point in even trying to make the sale or achieve your goal if it's not possible?* Suddenly, you find yourself wondering how you're ever going to find the next new marketer or sell another product, let alone reach the big goal you've been working toward.

I've been there many times, feeling deflated, thinking, *what's the point of even trying?* As a network marketer, if you're halfway through a month and you should be at $50,000 but you're only at $7,500, you begin to think, *There's no way I can make it.*

That's where extraordinary effort comes into play. You need to stay focused on your original goal—you need to connect to the vision you had for it, that big *why* you had in your heart and mind when you set the goal in the first place.

Like me, you need to reverse engineer the goal. Ask yourself, *If I'm at the end of this month and this goal were to have happened, what would I have done? What would I have needed to do?*

Whatever the answer, you will need to take massive action and give it everything you have, regardless of your results. You have to believe you can still ring the bell of success at the end. You have to maintain unwavering faith and extraordinary effort—until the buzzer sounds. That's the only way that you create an opportunity for the miracle to happen.

If you do what the average person does—what our built-in human nature tells us to do—you'll be just like every other average network marketer. Don't choose to be that average person! Remember: your thoughts and actions become a self-fulfilling prophecy.

Allow me to introduce you to your edge—the strategy that, when you use it, will skyrocket your goals and practically ensure every one of your ambitions is realized.

The Miracle Equation

Unwavering Faith + Extraordinary Effort = Miracles

It's easier than you think. The secret to maintaining unwavering faith is to recognize that it's a mindset and a *strategy*—it's not concrete. In fact, it's elusive. You can never make *every* sale. No athlete makes *every* shot. So, you have to program yourself to automatically have the unwavering faith to drive you to keep putting forth the extraordinary effort.

Remember, the key to putting this equation into practice, to maintaining unwavering faith in the midst of self-doubt, is the Miracle Mantra:

I will _____, no matter what. There is no other option.

For me recently, it was "My team will grow by 50 people this year, no matter what. There is no other option."

Once you set a goal, put that goal into the Miracle Mantra format. Yes, you're going to say your affirmations every morning (and maybe every evening, too). But all day, every day, you're going to repeat your Miracle Mantra to yourself. As you're driving or taking the train to the office, while you're on the treadmill, in the shower, in line at the grocery story, driving to pick up a prospect—in other words: *everywhere you go.*

Your Miracle Mantra will fortify your faith and be the self-talk you need to make just one more call or talk to one more person as they come through the door.

Bonus Lesson

Remember what I learned from my mentor, Dan Casetta: *The purpose of a goal isn't to hit the goal. The real purpose is to develop yourself into the type of person who can achieve your goals, regardless of whether you hit that particular one or not. It is who you become, by giving it everything you have until the last moment—regardless of your results—that matters most.*

You have to become the type of person who *can* achieve the goal. You won't always reach the goal, but you can become someone who maintains unwavering faith and puts forth extraordinary effort, regardless of your results. That's how you become the type of person you need to become to consistently achieve extraordinary goals.

And while reaching the goal almost doesn't matter (almost!), more often than not, you'll reach your goal. Do the elite athletes win every time? No. But they win most of the time. And you'll win most of the time, too.

At the end of the day, you can wake up earlier, do the Life S.A.V.E.R.S. with passion and excitement, get organized, focused, and intentional, and master every sales technique like a champ. And yet, if you don't combine unwavering faith with extraordinary effort, you won't reach the levels of sales success you seek.

The Miracle Equation gives you access to forces outside of anyone's understanding, using an energy that I might call God, the Universe, the Law of Attraction, or even good luck. I don't know how it works; I just know that it works.

You've read this far—you clearly want success more than almost anything. Commit to following through with every aspect of selling, including The Miracle Equation. You deserve it, and I want you to have it!

Putting It into Action:

Write out the Miracle Equation and put it where you will see it every day: **Unwavering Faith + Extraordinary Effort = Miracles (UF + EE = M∞)**

What's your #1 goal for this year? What goal, if you were to accomplish it, would take your success to a whole new level?

Write your Miracle Mantra: *I will* _____ *(insert your goals and daily actions, here), no matter what. There is no other option.*

It is more about who you become in the process. You'll expand your self-confidence and, regardless of your results, the very next time you attempt to reach a goal, and every time after that, you'll be the type of person who gives it all they've got.

Closing Remarks

Congratulations! You have done what only a small percentage of people do: read an entire book. If you've come this far, that tells me something about you: you have a thirst for more. You want to become more, do more, contribute more, and earn more.

Right now, you have the unprecedented opportunity to infuse the Life S.A.V.E.R.S. into your daily life and business, upgrade your daily routine, and ultimately upgrade your *life* to a first class experience beyond your wildest dreams. Before you know it, you will be reaping the astronomical benefits of the habits that top achievers use daily.

Five years from now, your life, business, relationships, and income will be a direct result of one thing: *who you've become*. It's up to you to wake up each day and dedicate time to becoming the best version of yourself. Seize this moment in time, define a vision for your future, and use what you've learned in this book to turn your vision into your reality.

Imagine a time just a few years from now when you come across the journal you started after completing this book. In it, you find the goals you wrote down for yourself—dreams you didn't even dare speak out loud at the time. And as you look around, you realize *your dreams now represent the life you are living*.

Right now, you stand at the foot of a mountain you can easily and effortlessly climb. All you need to do is continue waking up each day for your Miracle Morning and use the Life S.A.V.E.R.S. day after day, month after month, year after year, as you continue to take your *self*, your *business*, and your *success* to levels beyond what you've ever experienced before.

Combine your Miracle Morning with a commitment to master your Network Marketing Mastery Skills, and use The Miracle Equation to create results that most people only dream of.

This book was written as an expression of what Hal and I know will work for you, to take every area of your life to the next level, faster than you may currently believe is possible. Miraculous performers weren't born that way—they have simply dedicated their lives to developing themselves and their skills to achieve everything they've ever wanted.

You can become one of them, I promise.

Taking Action: The 30-Day Miracle Morning Challenge

Now it is time to join the tens of thousands of people who have transformed their lives, incomes, and network marketing careers with *The Miracle Morning*. Join the community online at TMMBook.com and download the toolkit to get you started *today.*

TOP ONE PERCENT NETWORKER INTERVIEW

Evan Klassen

www.EvanKlassen.com

Facebook.com/evan.klassen

LinkedIn.com/in/evanklassen

Twitter: @evanklassenvip

Instagram: @evanklassenvip

Evan was born in the mid 1980s in the poorest country in central Asia during war, poverty and persecution in a highly communistic country. Being one of nine children in a blue-collar working family taught him to work hard for everything in life.

After moving to Germany as a child, he began working for himself at age 11 to help support the family and have money for his own expenses.

Evan was 21 years old when he was introduced to Network Marketing and personal growth. To date, he has invested well over $120K into books, seminars, events, audio trainings and personal coaching because he believes the best investment you can make is an investment in yourself.

In 2006, Evan moved to the United States he started a real estate business. Through many struggles and persistence he grew the business from zero to over $22 million in revenue in a period of 4.5 years.

Evan has to traveled to 25 countries and inspired tens of thousands of people to pursue their dream. In 2008, he started his Network Marketing career in the USA and has built sales organizations with over 45,000 distributors in 23 countries with tens of millions in sales. He made his first million dollars as an entrepreneur by the age of 28

Evan is a best-selling author of two books that he co-authored: *Think and Grow Rich today* with Napoleon Hill and *Transform* with Brian Tracy. His passion is to help people to live Happy! He gives

Glory to God for all and, yes, network marketing has changed his life.

Evan's Miracle Morning & Daily Rituals:

- Every night I plan the next day before it begins so I can start my day with intention and focus.

- I get up around 7am in the morning and listen to personal growth podcasts and audiobooks for the first 30 minutes while getting ready for the gym.

- I work out for about 45 min, 3 -4 times per week while listening to personal growth audios.

- After the gym, I do what I call a Power Visual Mastermind for 30 minutes. This is something I created where I visualize myself in a meeting with ten people that I consider to be the brightest minds in different areas of my life. I visualize myself asking them for advice in their areas of expertise and I picture how they would respond. For example, Steve Jobs is my adviser on always staying ahead of the game and always innovating in life and business. Warren Buffett is my adviser on finances and investments. Dexter Yager is my adviser to my network marketing business. This mastermind allows me to tap into infinite creativity and power and I can envision and learn from the best people who live or lived.

- I do about 30 min of social media around 10:30am EST as this is one of the best times to post content.

- I always leave some time open for unexpected calls and business. In network marketing, there are always a lot of unexpected calls and opportunities to help the team!

- I try to be in bed by 10:30pm where I do some journaling about how my day was and experiences I had. (I use the app DayOne it's amazing for that!)

- Saturday is mostly a play day to catch up on fun and personal growth as well as strategize for business and life.

- On Sunday evenings, I plan my week before the week begins.

BONUS INTERVIEW FOR *MIRACLE MORNING FOR NETWORK MARKETING* READERS

Each of the Top One Percent Networkers that are featured in this book were interviewed by Pat Petrini about not only their morning routines, but their tips, techniques and strategies that have been critical in helping them become the best of the best in network marketing.

For your free and exclusive interview with Evan, go to www. TMMforNetworkMarketers.com/Evan

A Special Invitation from Hal

Readers and practitioners of *The Miracle Morning* have co-created an extraordinary community consisting of over 200,000 like-minded individuals from around the world who wake up each day with purpose and dedicate time to fulfilling the unlimited potential that is within all of us, while helping others to do the same.

As author of *The Miracle Morning*, I felt I had a responsibility to create an online community where readers could come together to connect, get encouragement, share best practices, support one another, discuss the book, post videos, find accountability partners, and even swap smoothie recipes and exercise routines.

However, I honestly had no idea that The Miracle Morning Community would become one of the most positive, engaged, and supportive online communities in the world—but it has. I'm constantly astounded by the caliber and character of our membership, which presently includes people from over 70 countries and is growing daily.

Just go to **www.MyTMMCommunity.com** and request to join The Miracle Morning Community on Facebook®. You'll immediately be able to connect with 80,000+ people who are already practicing TMM. While you'll find many who are just beginning their Miracle Morning journey, you'll discover even more who have been at it for years and who will happily share advice and guidance to accelerate your success.

I'll be moderating the Community and checking in regularly, so I look forward to seeing you there! If you'd like to reach out to me personally on social media, follow **@HalElrod** on Twitter and **Facebook.com/YoPalHal** on Facebook. Let's connect soon!

THANK YOU TO ALL OF OUR *TOP ONE PERCENT* NETWORK MARKETING INTERVIEWEES

Ann Sieg

Ana Gabriel Mann

Cindy Samuelson

Evan Klassen

Jennifer Glacken

Jessica Ellerman

Jordan Adler

Jordan Hubbard Monroe

Justin Prince

Keala Kanae

Lisa Cox

Maria Williams

Mark Hoverson

Ray Higdon

Rob Robson

Tanya Aliza

Todd Falcone

Vincent Ortega Jr.

ABOUT THE AUTHORS

HAL ELROD is on a mission to *Elevate the Consciousness of Humanity, One Morning at a Time.* As one of the highest rated keynote speakers in the America, creator of one of the fastest growing and most engaged online communities in existence and author of one of the highest rated books in the world, *The Miracle Morning*—which has been translated into 27 languages, has over 2,000 five-star Amazon reviews and is practiced daily by over 500,000 people in 70+ countries—he is doing exactly that.

The seed for Hal's life's work was planted at age twenty, when Hal was found dead at the scene of a horrific car accident. Hit head-on by a drunk driver at seventy miles per hour, he broke eleven bones, died for six minutes, and suffered permanent brain damage. After six days in a coma, he woke to face his unimaginable reality—which included being told by doctors that he would never walk again. Defying the logic of doctors and proving that all of us can overcome even seemingly insurmountable adversity to achieve anything we set our minds to, Hal went on to not only walk but to run a 52-mile ultramarathon and become a hall of fame business achiever—all before the age of 30.

Then, in November of 2016, Hal nearly died again. With his kidneys, lungs, and heart of the verge of failing, he was diagnosed with a very rare, very aggressive form of leukemia and given a 30% chance of living. After enduring the most difficult year of his life, Hal is now cancer-free and furthering his mission as the Executive Producer of *The Miracle Morning Movie.*

Most importantly, Hal is beyond grateful to be sharing his life with the woman of his dreams, Ursula Elrod, and their two children in Austin, Texas.

For more information on Hal's keynote speaking, live events, books, the movie and more, visit www.HalElrod.com.

Out of high school, **PAT PETRINI** began working with an international direct-sales company. He quickly rose through the ranks breaking numerous sales records and eventually became the top producer in the company out of tens of thousands of other reps.From there, Pat partnered with a leading network marketing company and became the youngest ranking leader to build an organization of thousands of people around the world generating millions of dollars in annual product sales.Pat has been selected as one of the "Top Mentors" in the direct-selling industry by a leading industry publication, he has spoken internationally to crowds of thousands and he has consulted with many network marketing companies on compensation plan design, duplication model development and field development strategies. He and his wife, Emily, also operate a successful real estate investment company that specializes in both short-term and long-term investment property and Pat runs an online course that teaches people how to build wealth through real estate investment. **For more information on Pat and the projects he is currently involved with, please visit www.PatPetrini.com.**

HONORÉE CORDER is the author of dozens of books, including *You Must Write a Book*, *The Prosperous Writers* book series, *Like a Boss* book series, *Vision to Reality*, *Business Dating*, *The Successful Single Mom* book series, *If Divorce is a Game, These are the Rules*, and *The Divorced Phoenix*. She is also Hal Elrod's business partner in *The Miracle Morning* book series. Honorée coaches business professionals, writers, and aspiring non-fiction authors who want to publish their books to bestseller status, create a platform, and develop multiple streams of income. She also does all sorts of other magical things, and her badassery is legendary. You can find out more at HonoreeCorder.com.

BOOK HAL TO SPEAK!

Book Hal As Your Keynote Speaker and You're Guaranteed to Make Your Event Highly Enjoyable & Unforgettable!

For more than a decade, Hal Elrod has been consistently rated as the #1 Keynote Speaker by meeting planners and attendees. His unique style combines inspiring audiences with his unbelieveable TRUE story, keeping them laughing hysterically with his high energy, stand-up comedy style delivery, and empowering them with actionable strategies to take their RESULTS to the next level.

"Hal received a 9.8 out of 10 from our members. That never happens."
–Entrepreneur Organization (NYC Chapter)

"Hal was the featured keynote speaker for 400 of our top sales performers and executive team. He gave us a plan that was so simple, we had no choice but to put it into action immediately."
–Art Van Furniture

"Bringing Hal in to be the keynote speaker at our annual conference was the best investment we could have made."
–Fidelity National Title

For More Info - Visit www.HalElrod.com

THE MIRACLE MORNING SERIES

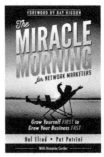

The Journal

for Salespeople

for Real Estate Agents

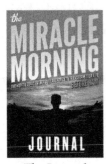

for Network Marketers

for Writers

for Entrepreneurs

for Parents & Families

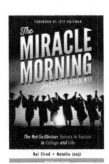

for College Students

COMPANION GUIDES & WORKBOOKS

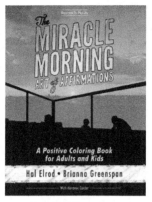

Art of Affirmations

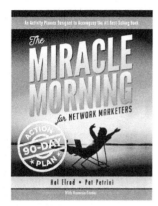

**for Network Marketers
90-Day Action Plan**

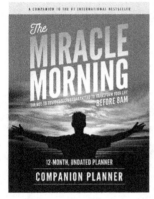

Companion Planner

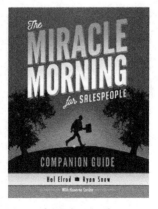

**for Salespeople
Companion Guide**

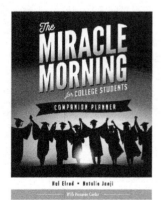

**for College Students
Companion Planner**

HAL ELROD & JON BERGHOFF

PRESENT...

ONE WEEKEND CAN CHANGE YOUR LIFE.
JOIN US FOR THIS ONCE-IN-A-LIFETIME EXPERIENCE.

www.BestYearEverLive.com

Most personal development events cause "information overload" and often leave attendees feeling more overwhelmed than when they arrived. You end up with pages and pages of notes, then you go home and have to figure out how and when to implement everything you've learned.

Co-hosted by experiential trainer, Jon Berghoff, the **Best Year Ever Blueprint LIVE** event won't just teach you how to change your life, you'll actually starting taking steps to *change your life while you're still at the event*.

"I truly had a life changing weekend during BYEB2015. I feel as if my mind has hit a 'reset' button. Reading The Miracle Morning and coming to the live event has been a gift, and the best investment in myself I've ever made. I am excited to take this momentum and create my level 10 life next year!"

Ericka Staples

Learn more about the Best Year Ever event online at
WWW.BESTYEAREVERLIVE.COM